*The*
*Connell Guide*
*to*
*Thomas Hardy's*

_____

# Far from the
# Madding Crowd

_____

*by*
*Phillip Mallett*

# Contents

# NOTES

# Introduction

*Far from the Madding Crowd* marked a turning point in Thomas Hardy's career: his fourth published novel, but the first to be both a critical and a popular success. It was commissioned by Leslie Stephen, editor of the prestigious *Cornhill Magazine*, who had enjoyed the rural scenes in Hardy's second and most harmonious book, *Under the Greenwood Tree*, and thought *Cornhill* readers – for the most part middle-class, educated and urban – might welcome something similar. In response, Hardy offered him a "pastoral tale" in which "the chief characters would probably be a young woman-farmer, a shepherd, and a sergeant of cavalry".

He had played safe in *Under the Greenwood Tree*, and may have intended to do so again, with a story turning on romantic and marital choice. In the hands of most authors, the courtship plot was a conservative form, in which the heroine, though fickle or inexperienced enough to be tempted to choose the wrong man, learns from her errors in time to marry the right one at the end. "What should a woman do with her life?" asks the narrator of Anthony Trollope's *Can You Forgive Her?* (1865), before answering his question in the way readers of Victorian fiction came to expect: "Fall in love, marry the man, have two children, and live happy ever afterwards."

Hardy could certainly claim that he had given Stephen what he wanted, in a series of scenes devoted to sheep-shearing and harvest suppers, saving hayricks from fire and battling against storms, all leavened with a rustic humour which risks but stops short of caricature, and honouring both the skills of the workfolk (a term Hardy preferred to "labourers") and the sense of community that builds around them.

For better or worse – Hardy later grumbled that he had "not the slightest intention of writing for ever about sheep-farming" – *Far from the Madding Crowd* was the novel Victorian readers wanted him to write over and over. Andrew Lang, reviewing it in the *Academy*, was delighted by the pastoral elements: "when the sheep are shorn in the ancient town of Weatherbury, the scene is one that Shakespeare or that Chaucer might have watched. It is this immobile rural existence that the novelist has to paint." Over the next century and more, numerous critics, publishers and film-makers have followed Lang in reading Hardy as the historian and celebrant of an age in which the countryside was the wellspring of national greatness and the guardian of a quintessential Englishness: a world enduring, close-knit, self-sufficient, all but timeless.

But as critics such as John Goode, Raymond Williams and Linda Shires have pointed out, it requires considerable ideological wrenching to see *Far from the Madding Crowd* as a true romance of country life, undisturbed by economic pressures and patriarchal sexual politics. As was to happen more than once over the next 20 years, what Hardy had promised as a quiet story suitable for family reading took off in unexpected directions. Bathsheba is not merely tempted to make the wrong choice, but does so, and is only saved from the lifelong consequences of her mistake when a third suitor, Farmer Boldwood, murders the husband who torments her. Rather than a "pastoral tone and idyllic simplicity", noted a critic in the *Westminster Review,* what marked *Far from the Madding Crowd* was its "violent sensationalism": marital desertion, illegitimacy, death in childbirth, murder, attempted suicide and insanity. If there was much that Leslie Stephen might have welcomed, there was much too to make him uneasy.

Yet this is not a dark novel. Nearly 30 years

STEPHEN'S
RED PENCIL

The manuscript evidence of *Far from the Madding Crowd* shows Leslie Stephen regularly red pencilling Hardy's text, on occasions as an experienced editor dealing with a young author who aimed to be "a good hand at a serial", but just as often to protect the *Cornhill*'s readers. Some of

after its publication, Hardy wrote that it seemed to him "like the work of a youngish hand, though perhaps there is something in it which I could not have put there had I been older". That "something" has been variously identified as charm, amplitude, richness of incident and humour, the evocation of landscape and the rhythms of the work that shaped it, or, more broadly, the assurance that despite the sense that deep social and economic changes are imminent, the novel still holds out the possibility that the closing marriage will maintain the community and its traditional order a little longer.

All these elements are indeed present in the novel, and are a source of its continuing appeal. If even here, in the last work he was to write from his childhood home in Bockhampton, Hardy could not wholly ignore the darker aspects of rural life, *Far from the Madding Crowd* remains the warmest and most celebratory of farewells.

---

the resulting changes were trivial, as when "the buttocks and tails of half a dozen warm and contented horses" became "backs and tails". Others were more significant.

Stephen warned Hardy to treat the seduction of Fanny Robin in "a gingerly fashion", adding that he would "be glad to omit the baby" from the scene in which Bathsheba opens Fanny's coffin. Similar wary negotiations between author and editor were to mark much of Hardy's career until, after *Jude the Obscure* (1895), he lost patience, gave up novel-writing, and returned to poetry ■

# A summary of the plot

Gabriel Oak, who by thrift and hard work has raised himself from shepherd to farmer, proposes marriage to the beautiful and spirited Bathsheba Everdene. She refuses him, and moves away to run a farm inherited from her uncle. Soon after, an inexperienced sheep dog drives Gabriel's flock over a cliff, leaving him ruined. He finds work on Bathsheba's farm, again as a shepherd, though for her sake he also acts as an unofficial farm bailiff.

In an idle moment Bathsheba sends a Valentine's card to a reserved local farmer, Boldwood, a man twice her age, but the joke misfires when he falls obsessively in love with her. A sense of obligation makes her feel she should marry him, but before she commits herself she falls for the handsome Sergeant Troy. Unknown to her, Troy has previously seduced and was about to marry one of her servants, Fanny Robin, until a misunderstanding caused the wedding to be abandoned. Rejecting the advice of the loyal Gabriel, and against her own better judgement, Bathsheba marries Troy.

The marriage soon proves unsuccessful, and collapses completely when Fanny returns to the area. She dies in childbirth; Bathsheba discovers her identity, and her connection with Troy, beside the coffin which contains both Fanny and her baby. Almost at once Troy leaves the area and is believed drowned, prompting Boldwood to renew his suit.

Worn down, Bathsheba agrees to marry him once the law allows her to do so, seven years after Troy's disappearance. But Troy has in fact returned, and on the night of a Christmas party at which Boldwood hopes to announce his engagement to Bathsheba, he enters to reclaim her as his wife. She screams; Boldwood shoots him, and tries to kill himself. Prevented from doing so, he walks to the jail, and is eventually confined for life as of unsound mind. A year later, the chastened Bathsheba hints to Oak that he should propose again; this time she accepts him, and they marry in "the most private, secret, plainest wedding that it is possible to have".

# What is *Far from the Madding Crowd* about?

For many readers, the "very short and simple" subject of *Far from the Madding Crowd* (in Henry James's phrase) is the maturation of Bathsheba Everdene, from what James described with evident distaste as "a young lady of the inconsequential, wilful, mettlesome type... which aims at giving one a very intimate sense of a young lady's *womanishness*", to a woman with a renewed sense of social and personal responsibility, as she gradually surrenders to the "integrity and simplicity and sturdy patience" of Gabriel Oak. Most recent critics have come to the same conclusion. Robert Langbaum views the novel as "a traditionally comic 'taming of the shrew' story". Alan Friedman speaks of Bathsheba's "taming", and her "cutting down to size" as a necessary "containment". Peter Casagrande traces a similar dynamic, but argues that despite her "severe schooling" by the events of the novel, Bathsheba is incapable of real amendment. Rosemarie Morgan picks up on the hints of misogyny that underlie at least some of these views (and in Casagrande's opinion are to be found in Hardy himself), but rather than development sees loss and diminution, as Hardy's

## OUR FIRST GLIMPSE OF BATHSHEBA

Hardy's approach to the craft of fiction can be briefly illustrated from the first chapter of *Far from the Madding Crowd*. Alone on a wagon, unaware that she is being observed by Gabriel Oak, Bathsheba – her name is not yet known to us – opens a small swing mirror, and gazes into it; she parts her lips, and smiles:

*What possessed her to indulge in such a performance in sight of the sparrows, blackbirds and unperceived farmer, who*

vibrant, self-delighting, energetic heroine... blossoms into womanhood, ventures into business, into marriage, into the world of men, and is nullified. And Hardy is the lone mourner.

There is clearly some justice in these readings. The narrator appears to endorse them in his description of the "substantial affection" which arises between Oak and Bathsheba as "romance growing up in the interstices of hard prosaic reality". Commenting on these opposing terms, Roy Morrell thinks that the novel "disparages romance, the dream and the dreamer", as embodied in Boldwood's unreal conception of Bathsheba, or her vision of Troy ("brilliant in brass and scarlet"), or Troy's idealisation of the dead

*were alone its spectators – whether the smile began as a factitious one to test her capacity in that art – nobody knows; it ended certainly in a real smile; she blushed at herself, and seeing her reflection blush, blushed the more.*

There are three perspectives here. Gabriel, the named observer, draws the "cynical inference" that the young woman is vain. The anonymous narrator, in apparent agreement, remarks on "woman's prescriptive infirmity", before going on to associate the smiles with thoughts of future triumphs in love, and hearts lost and won. But the point of view which matters most is the one we are explicitly denied, in the small intimate space between Bathsheba's eyes and the smiling and blushing face that she but not we can see in the mirror. As if to

Fanny Robin (the chapter on the planting of her grave is called "Troy's Romanticism"), and suggests instead that one should live "in accordance with reality", as Gabriel learns to do. Discussing the idea that Oak also develops, Irving Howe is another critic who sees the novel in terms of a broader social discipline: the melodramatic excesses of "unfocused human desire" – variously, Bathsheba's "feminine wilfullness", Oak's "unmanly patience", Boldwood's "sickened love", and Troy's "vanity" – are made to yield to "the discipline of civilization", as represented in the hard work and responsibility of running a farm. Howe is among a number of critics to emphasise the importance of work in Hardy's fiction: men and women have always worked, but Hardy is the first great novelist to show them doing so side by side.

acknowledge our uncertainty ("nobody knows" why she chose to look in the mirror at this moment), the narrator withdraws his implicit claim to be able to speak for her: "the whole series of actions was so idly put forth as to make it rash to assert that intention had any part in them at all". Gabriel too, a moment later, gives up "his point of espial". Scrutiny, speculation, generalisation, all fail to explain the woman's actions; we are left with an image of unabashed self-delight, about which we can make no final judgement. The privacy on which the reader has broken is restored to her.

This variety of angles of vision might be said to dramatise one of the issues of the novel: the attempt by three different men to impose an identity, and their own name, on Bathsheba. Here

To see the novel as a study of passion modulating into sobriety, of the value of work as a means of self-definition, and of the sustaining power of the human community, is wholly reasonable. It also allows room to appreciate what Michael Millgate calls the "extraordinary amplitude" of the novel, felt in the profusion of incident, the richness of description, and the humour of the rustic dialogue. But an account of *Far from the Madding Crowd* on these lines misses the felt intensity of many of its scenes.

Such readings are not "wrong" – it would be remarkable if they were, and the novel were held to advocate *not* living "in accordance with reality" – but they fail to account for its power. Consider, for example, the final sentences of Chapter 28, 'The Hollow amid the Ferns', after Troy's sword display:

she is allowed to elude the efforts of both Oak and the narrator to intercept her self-contemplation, and to reduce her smiles and blushes to ready-made maxims about female vanity.

But we read against the grain of the chapter if we construe it as the novelist's initial statement of an "idea", or what Henry James termed the *donnée*. What we take from the scene is that the watching farmer and the woman with the crimson jacket will repay our attention. Hardy offers us the undervalued pleasures of "story": the question of what will happen next between this man and this woman, timed by the gradually diminishing number of pages between our right thumb and forefinger. As Ian Gregor puts it, succinctly: "The novel lies open before us." ■

*That minute's interval had brought the blood*
*beating into her face, set her stinging as if aflame to*
*the very hollows of her feet, and enlarged emotion to*
*a compass which quite swamped thought. It had*
*brought upon her a stroke resulting, as did that of*
*Moses in Horeb, in a liquid stream – here a stream of*
*tears. She felt like one who has sinned a great sin.*

*The circumstance had been the gentle dip of Troy's*
*mouth downwards upon her own. He had kissed her.*

It is easy enough to make this chapter fit into a
moral scheme: Bathsheba is wilful and even
irresponsible in meeting Troy alone; Troy's
brilliance with the sword contrasts both with
Gabriel's momentary clumsiness when he nips the
ewe with his shears, and the skill he exhibits in
saving the sheep with his trochar (a form of
'lance'); the dazzling movements of the sword,
"quick as electricity", find an echo in the lightning
and thunder of the summer storm, which
Bathsheba, in this instance working alongside Oak
rather than made to stand motionless, again bears
"without flinching". Yet these structural parallels
are less striking than the moment itself.

Troy's kiss releases feelings in Bathsheba that
neither she nor the reader yet knew she was
capable of, let alone held in check. It also prompts
a dizzying sense of "sin", which reaches far beyond
such terms as "vanity" or "wilfulness". Why she
feels as she does – whether it is the sense that her

Thomas Hardy, *portrait by Reginald Grenville Eves, oil on canvas, 1923*

life is about to undergo a transformation, or fear that she has been untrue to herself, or a premonition that Troy will prove faithless – is a question it will take the rest of the novel to resolve.

The critic who has come closest to this aspect of Hardy's work is D.H. Lawrence, in his brilliant if one-eyed *Study of Thomas Hardy*. Written in 1914 in a rage against the "colossal idiocy" of the Great War, it would, he said, "be about anything but Thomas Hardy", but at its core it is an exploration of how Hardy imagines the self in relation to what Lawrence elsewhere calls "the circumambient universe". Lawrence argues that Hardy is divided between a gloomy "metaphysic", derived from his preconceived theories *about* life and its inevitable pains, and his "sensuous understanding" – the intuitions *of* life that he discovers in the process of writing his novels. The former encourages him to

## HOW TO READ HARDY

Hardy described himself as one of those whose "natures become vocal at tragedy", and it is tempting to read back through such later works as *Tess of the d'Urbervilles* and *Jude the Obscure*, and to see the potentially tragic elements in *Madding Crowd* as signs of the "real" Hardy. It would be nearer the mark to describe the Hardy of the 1870s as an experimental novelist: *Desperate Remedies* was a sensation novel, *A Pair of Blue Eyes* a romance, *The*

bring his heroes and heroines to disaster; the latter leads him to recognise, as no English novelist before him, that "the centre, the turning pivot" of a man's life is his sex life – and one might add that for Hardy, unlike earlier novelists, this is as true of women as of men.

According to Lawrence, human life is caught between "the Law" and "Love": that is, between the need for "self-preservation" – which includes a willingness to admit the demands of the community, work and family – and the need to follow the sexual instinct. Hardy's greatness is to see that in the last analysis the sex instinct is prior to and more compelling than any other. In Lawrence's words, the "final aim of every living thing, creature, or being is the full achievement of itself":

Hand of Ethelberta a "Comedy in Chapters", *The Trumpet-Major* an historical novel, and so on.

Of the first nine novels, only one, *The Return of the Native*, aims unequivocally at tragedy. More often, Hardy breaks generic boundaries. In *Far from the Madding Crowd*, as the reviewers noticed, there are both pastoral and sensational elements. It might equally be seen as a tragicomedy, with two competing strands: one where the human capacity to cause and endure hurt and disaster is followed through to its tragic conclusion, and another where suffering brings maturity, and a chastened version of the "comic" happy ending in the final marriage.

It's understandable to

What exactly the struggle into being consists in, is the question. But most obviously... the first and chiefest factor is the struggle into love and the struggle with love: by love, meaning the love of a man for a woman and a woman for a man. The *via media* to being, for man or woman, is love, and love alone.

The deliberate purposes of the intellect, like the moral systems agreed by communities, are part of human life, but only a part. Those who focus on the systems are trying to live as if a map of the surface was a true picture of human life, whereas "the greater part of every life is underground, like roots in the dark in contact with the beyond". The notion of the "beyond", and of the sexual life as a means of entering into it, is of course one of Lawrence's main concerns as a novelist, and the point of

smooth out the discontinuities, to look for "organic" coherence and generic stability, but to do so is to diminish the novel, and to interpret as faults what might better be seen as typical Hardian strengths.

As Ian Gregor has argued, it is rarely helpful to stand back and seek "a total view" of a Hardy novel. One might, for example, see *Far from the Madding Crowd* as a study of the opposing values of rural and urban ways of life, or of the need to balance passion (represented by Troy) with sobriety, good sense and hard work (represented by Gabriel). Such accounts are not mistaken, but as we read they seem beside the point. We do better, in Gregor's words, to see the novel "not as a pattern which defines itself,

connection between his own work and Hardy's.

Michael Herbert has argued for the profound influence of Lawrence's *Study* on later readings of Hardy, especially in its rejection of conventionally moral approaches. In Lawrence's terms, those critics who read *Far from the Madding Crowd* as a book about the necessary moral education of Bathsheba are attending to the metaphysics of the novel at the expense of its sensuous understanding. His own summary has a very different emphasis:

> Sergeant Troy treats Bathsheba badly, never loves her, though he is the only man in the book who knows anything about her... Troy is killed by Boldwood... enter the good, steady Gabriel, who marries Bathsheba because he will make her a good husband, and the flower of imaginative love is dead for her with Troy's scorn of her.

but as a gradually unfolding process", and recognise that "the novel is different things at different times".

It is entirely legitimate for, say, Henry James, to aim at textural unity, a consistent position for the narrator, and the subordination of every element in the text to a central concern. But this is not Hardy's procedure. He valued the "provisional" over the consistent, and what he called "a series of seemings" over the effort to resolve "series" into oneness; he delighted in expressive "disproportion", shifts of perspective, and an authorial voice which is sometimes that of an omniscient narrator, at others that of a witness moved to comment on events as if they were being enacted before him ∎

On this account, the novel is about the "flower of imaginative love", and its destruction; what it most seeks to explore is not Oak's steadiness, but whatever it is that Troy "knows" about Bathsheba, and which leads her to marry him.

Lawrence's *Study* is tendentious as well as illuminating, especially in treating love and sexual desire as if they were timeless universals, whereas in Hardy's novels, as indeed in Lawrence's own, they are mediated through class and social distance. But he is surely right to insist that "the struggle into love" is at the centre of the Wessex novels. *Far from the Madding Crowd* is "about" many things – among them, work, the rural community, class mobility and social change – but pre-eminently it is about love and desire: what love is, how it arises, and what sustains it; what causes it to fail or disappoint, and on what terms it permits the man and the woman to come into being. Despite Lawrence's too-ready dismissal of him, "good, steady Gabriel" voices the imperative that drives all of Hardy's major characters: "I shall do one thing in this life – one thing certain – that is, love you, and long for you, and *keep wanting* you till I die" (4).* What that means – how it feels to love and to want – is the real subject of the novel.

*\* Throughout this book, the numbers in brackets refer to the chapters from which the quotations are taken.*

# Is Boldwood mad?

Farmer Boldwood seems not to have been part of Hardy's original conception of *Far from the Madding Crowd*. In narrative terms, his role is to be Troy's rival in the middle part of the novel, by which time Gabriel has been reduced to Bathsheba's shepherd rather than her suitor, but he quickly becomes much more than that: a disturbed and dangerous man, and the first near-tragic figure in Hardy's fiction. He enters the novel as an off-stage voice, asking for news of Fanny Robin and replying "indifferently" when told that Bathsheba is too busy to see him.

This indifference is repeated when he takes no notice of Bathsheba on her debut at the Casterbridge corn-market, and later passes her on the road without even a side-glance in her direction. Liddy remarks that "Men be such a terrible class of society to look at a body," (12) but looking at Bathsheba is just what Boldwood, buried in his own reserve, initially refuses to do, and it is pique at this lack of interest that prompts her to send him the valentine. Almost instantly he becomes obsessed with her, and she spends much of the rest of the novel trying to evade his gaze or escape his conversation. The psychological power associated with looking, the unease that comes of being looked at, and the relation of the gaze to gender and to social class are among the central concerns of *Far from the Madding Crowd*.

The chapters leading up to Boldwood's proposal of marriage raise questions about his stability, but offer uncertain answers. There is no doubt that the valentine disturbs him. The red seal, "Marry Me", becomes like "a blot of blood in the retina of his eye"; he scrutinises the writing with the intensity of a fetishist, mentally tracing the hand which had "travelled softly over the paper", linking the curves of the letters to the way the author's lips had "curved" with their "natural tremulousness" (14). But his pursuit of Bathsheba doesn't originate in sexual desire; he even has to ask others whether she is considered beautiful. His is what Hardy calls, precisely, an "ideal passion": the passion of a man who is in love with an idea, with no basis in any reality outside himself.

His hitherto solitary existence has left him "without a channel of any kind for disposable emotion", and he has become "surcharged" with an excess of feeling; Bathsheba has opened "sluices of feeling" within him, and he is swept away in the ensuing flood. This language of hydraulics and electricity appears elsewhere in Hardy's fiction, suggesting that love is something like a medical condition, inviting scientific or material analysis. The implication is that romantic and sexual desire operates relentlessly, driven by its own momentum, and beyond the control of the lover. Certainly it is beyond Boldwood's.

Boldwood tells Bathsheba that he has never loved before, but the narrator half hints otherwise: there are "old floodmarks faintly visible", suggestive of "wild capabilities", though "he had never been seen at the high tides which caused them" (18). It seems improbable that he deliberately lies to Bathsheba; more likely, we are to assume that he has managed to bury whatever lies in his emotional past so effectively that he no longer has any sense of it. Hardy describes him as "trained to repression", anticipating by 20 years the term Freud was to use in his *Studies on Hysteria* to describe the involuntary psychological mechanism which keeps painful experiences from entering the consciousness.

Freud's work began to appear in the mid-1890s, as Hardy was about to abandon fiction, and so came too late to influence him, but like Freud Hardy was fascinated by the paradoxical concept of "unconscious motivation": that is, those aims and impulses which drive action but are unknown even to those who act upon them. In Hardy's later novels, these are often revealed to the reader, though not to the agent, by coincidence or mistake; a familiar example is the letter of confession in *Tess of the d'Ubervilles*, which Tess pushes not only under Angel's door but also under his carpet, revealing her conflicting desires both to tell and to hide the truth. In *Far from the Madding Crowd* similar hidden currents of feeling are typically suggested by the landscape, or by what characters see, even when we are told little of what they deliberately think. After Boldwood has spent the night brooding on the valentine, the winter scene exhibits "the bond and slavery of frost", a world which appears as still and frozen as Boldwood himself, but beneath which the irresistible "bustlings, strainings, united thrusts" of the returning spring begin to "move and swell". That these energies are said to be more powerful than the cranes and pulleys at work in the city suggests

## THE TITLE

Far from the madding
    crowd's ignoble strife,
Their sober wishes never
    learn'd to stray;
Along the cool sequester'd
    vale of life
They kept the noiseless
    tenor of their way.

Hardy took his title from Thomas Gray's "Elegy Written in a Country Churchyard" (1750), one of the most popular poems of the 18th century. Gray's stanza refers to the men and women buried around the church, who kept their distance from the noise and ambition of the town (madding: frenzied, uncontrolled), and so lived a peaceful and decent life.

To be far from the madding crowd, then, is to belong to the countryside, and to live quietly and honestly. But if Hardy's title evokes the juxtaposition of two worlds, the rural and the

something mechanical, monstrous, about them. These are the forces Bathsheba has called into being in Boldwood.

Where he once ignored her, Boldwood now watches Bathsheba obsessively. When he next calls she is dressed in a new riding habit – "the first she had ever worn" in the manuscript, later revised to "the most elegant" – as she supervises the sheep-washing (19). She has become a respectable woman-farmer who oversees her workfolk and rides side-saddle: no longer the carefree young

urban, and implies the superiority of the former, the novel hardly endorses such a view: this particular vale of life overflows with strife (including murder), straying wishes (theft, seduction, obsession), and the "noise" of quarrels, recriminations and tears, as well as destitution, cruelty, the death of livestock, and actual madness. Gray's pastoral dream is, it seems, being exposed as an artifice, an ideal derived from literary tradition and not from observable reality.

Yet, as usual in Hardy, a simple either/or reading proves inadequate. Gray's literary pastoral is rejected, but in its place Hardy offers what might be termed "realist pastoral": a vision which acknowledges the potential harshness and pain of rural life, but suggests that these can be accommodated within the community.

Gabriel and Bathsheba are not blessed with "sober wishes" at the outset of the novel; they achieve them over the course of time, with difficulty, but finding support in the routines of rural labour. It is only in the closing pages of the novel that they enter on "the noiseless tenor of their way" ∎

woman once seen by Gabriel with her head draped over her horse's tail and her feet on its shoulders. But even this role allows her more freedom than Boldwood can bear to imagine. His proposal of marriage is only one step removed from the promise of imprisonment in a gilded cage; in the future he offers, the dairy superintendence will be done by others, and she will "never have so much as to look out of doors at haymaking time". Rather than ride on horseback, she is to have a genteel pony-carriage. His language is all in terms of his own needs: *want, win, protect, cherish, get, obtain.* She is a possession to be gained; what Bathsheba herself might want – whether she enjoys running a farm, or likes to look or indeed be outdoors – does not enter his mind.

The scene is echoed at the sheep-shearing in the Great Barn, but is made more complex by Gabriel's presence as both observed and observer. Again the text draws attention to the power of the look: initially, Bathsheba's supervisory gaze as Gabriel strips the sheep of its fleece, exposing the "pink flush" beneath – "She blushes at the insult," murmurs Bathsheba – followed by the evidence of Boldwood's masculine power over her, compelling her to look down "demurely" at a straw lying on the ground, as she in her turn becomes "red in the cheek", her blood "wavering in uncertain flux and reflux" (22). Bathsheba's gaze depends for its authority on her new class position, Boldwood's on his gender: Gabriel, whose "eyes could not forsake" them, is thus doubly unmanned, as employee and rejected lover. Thrown off-guard, he snips the ewe he is shearing in the groin, and is then himself wounded "in a still more vital part" by Bathsheba's rebuke. Unlike Boldwood, however, as subsequent scenes reveal, Gabriel can call on "manly resolve" to conceal his feelings.

Hardy's analysis of the power of the gaze, and of the hurt it can inflict, reaches its height in Chapter 31, titled 'Blame – Fury'. By now Troy has entered Bathsheba's life, and when Boldwood next approaches her it is he who is "looking at the ground". When he sees her, however, his look is "unanswerable", forcing her to turn aside before she can recover "self-possession" (given his desire to own her, the term is significant) and "fix" her eyes on him. In the scene that follows, Boldwood conceives himself the object of universal scorn: "the very hills and sky seem to laugh at me till I blush shamefully for my folly... if I had got jilted secretly, and the dishonour not known, and my position kept!" He becomes blind to Bathsheba's presence, and deaf to her pleadings ("He did not hear her at all now"). He is "living outside his defences... with a fearful sense of exposure".

The narrator comments that this is "the usual experience of strong natures when they love", but there is nothing usual here, and not much about love. What the scene reveals is the overwhelming desire of a damaged man to cling to a fantasy, of himself as the faithful lover who alone has the right to gaze on Bathsheba, and its terrifying corollary, in which the whole world laughs at the jilted man. Each vision is as fanciful and narcissistic as the other.

Chapter 34, titled 'Home Again – A Trickster', is a cruelly detailed account of what "exposure" might mean, as Troy plays with Boldwood's distress, first accepting money from him as a bribe to marry Fanny (see opposite), then more money to marry Bathsheba instead, before finally revealing that he has already married her, and throwing the money into the road. Troy is heartless, but right, when he points out that Boldwood, for all his professed love for Bathsheba, is ready to believe on the slightest evidence that she has sold herself "soul and body" to Troy. The "love" he asserts with such vehemence has no relation to her real existence; nothing she can do will either appease or deflect it. But neither does he have any insight into his own feelings, other than the sense of hurt and humiliation.

In retrospect, Boldwood can be seen to prefigure Henchard in *The Mayor of Casterbridge* – in his wrongheadedness, the volcanic nature of his passions, the pain of an apparently strong man broken down – but with the crucial difference that Henchard's growing love for his stepdaughter,

*Opposite: Troy (Terrence Stamp) accepts a bribe from Boldwood (Peter Finch) in John Schlesinger's 1967 film.*

Elizabeth-Jane, attaches him enough to reality and the community to hold out the possibility of his personal and social reintegration. With Boldwood there is nothing: even the task of running his farm fails to anchor him. Appropriately, Gabriel, who has been carefully "watching [Bathsheba's] affairs" – in both senses of the word – now takes over the "superintendence" of Boldwood's property. In an ironic twist, Boldwood finds himself reduced to the position of passive dependence he had offered Bathsheba.

What Hardy anatomises in Boldwood, then, is not love but pathology. This reaches its climax in the scene of his Christmas party, which sees the return of Troy, Boldwood's murder of him and his own attempted suicide, and then his steady march towards Casterbridge jail to await, as he hopes, execution. This last phase of the novel raises explicitly the question of Boldwood's sanity. In a passage added in the proofs to Chapter 35, before publication in the *Cornhill*, Troy asks Jan Coggan, with apparent casualness, "if insanity has ever appeared in Mr Boldwood's family"; to which Coggan replies with a vague memory of an uncle who was "queer in his head".

In Chapter 55, in all editions prior to the 1912 edition, the narrator reports that "Bathsheba and Troy, alone of all others", had suspected Boldwood of "mental derangement". In 1912, however, Hardy changed "Troy" to "Oak", even though the same chapter notes later that Oak's "conscience" tells him that Boldwood "ought to die". This seems inconsistent, and suggests, against the grain of the novel, that Oak might only reluctantly have joined those "few merciful men" who petition for the shooting to be regarded as an "outcome of madness" rather than wilful murder. But it may be that Hardy wished to engage his readers in what was in the 1870s an active debate about how far insanity might be used as a legal defence, and the relation of this defence to a range of questions: the fact of extreme provocation, signs of monomania, traces of hereditary madness, or proof of earlier intentions (Boldwood has previously threatened to harm Troy).

All of these might be illustrated from the latter part of the novel, though for the modern reader the evidence of the dresses, muffs, jewellery and the like which Boldwood has collected, packed in paper, and labelled "Bathsheba Boldwood", seems reason enough to think him insane. Indeed, the nearest he comes to rational behaviour in the closing pages is in his wish to die, rather than to be detained in an asylum, where he will be exposed to the gaze of warders and doctors during Her Majesty's pleasure: an all too real fulfilment of his worst fears.

Is Boldwood mad? Hardy's fiction frequently turns on events which are complex in law (as, for example, Alec's rape/seduction of Tess, and her later murder of him), and in the case of Boldwood his interest may have been sharpened by the fact that James Fitzjames Stephen, brother of Leslie Stephen, had been involved as legal counsel in a recent high-profile case with some resemblance to Boldwood's story. In *Far from the Madding Crowd*, the judge and jury reach one verdict about Boldwood; the Home Secretary admits the possibility of another. The reader is left to decide.

But there is a wider issue, which engages readers of novels as well as jurors at a criminal trial. How far is it possible to infer a character's state of mind from his or her actions? To what extent are the minds of others knowable? Are there limits to our power of self-inspection? How (in effect) can we "read" character? The mid-and late-Victorian novel, as handled by George Eliot or Henry James, developed a variety of means – free indirect speech, the omniscient narrator, extended passages of self-reflection – to give at least the illusion that we can understand ourselves and others. Hardy, by contrast, was more concerned with what in each case we *fail* to know. His work, as he insisted on numerous occasions, offers only a "series of seemings". It deals in the 'provisional', not the definitive. There are moments of clumsiness in the creation of Boldwood – notably, a tendency to describe him in antitheses, as in the 'Meditation' section of Chapter 18 ("He was always hit mortally, or he was missed") – but he stands as the first attempt in Hardy's work to explore what was to become one of his crucial preoccupations: that we may never achieve full comprehension of our own natures, or the nature of others, any more than of the universe.

# Why does Bathsheba marry Sergeant Troy?

In Chapter 15, Gabriel Oak asks Boldwood: "What sort of a man is this Sergeant Troy?" It's a question Hardy himself found difficult to answer. Throughout his career, his male characters tend to fall into two broad types, one sexually confident and assertive, the other reticent or inhibited, at times pathologically so. The point is well made by H.M. Daleski, who notes that Hardy was "preoccupied with two opposed conceptions of male sexuality, fascinated and repelled by his rake figures and wary and sceptical of his sexually diffident heroes". In *Far from the Madding Crowd* Bathsheba marries a man of each kind, settling in the end for the unassuming Gabriel, but only after she has previously rejected him, and fallen hopelessly in love with the dangerous and seductive Sergeant Troy.

She and Troy first meet during her nightly inspection of the farm (24). The two collide in the dark; as she tries to regain her balance she strikes against "warm clothes and buttons" – the warmth neatly suggesting her awareness of the body within the clothes – and finds herself trapped as his spur catches in her dress:

> *"We have got hitched together somehow, I think."*
> *"Yes."*
> *"Are you a woman?"*
> *"Yes."*
> *"A lady, I should have said."*
> *"It doesn't matter."*
> *"I am a man."*
> *"Oh!"*

## VIRGINIA WOOLF'S VIEW

Virginia Woolf, the daughter of Leslie Stephen, noticed the sense of openness that marks Hardy's novels:

The novels are full of inequalities... there is always about them a little blur of unconsciousness, that halo of freshness and margin of the unexpressed which often produce the most profound sense of satisfaction. It is as if Hardy himself was not quite aware of what he did, as if his consciousness held more than he could produce, and he left it for his readers to make out his full meaning and to supplement it from their own experience ■

Troy immediately takes the initiative; Bathsheba is reduced to brief replies. She is, literally, "hooked", a "prisoner"; ominously, getting separated is "likely to be a matter of time". The forewarning of violence and penetration is evident – Richard Carpenter speaks of "the cruel potency" of Troy's spur cutting into soft fabric – but there is something else too: "A hand seized the lantern, the door was opened, the rays burst out from their prison." The vigour of the verbs, and the metaphor of light escaping from a prison, suggest liberation as well as entrapment. In place of the darkness, Troy stands revealed, "brilliant in brass and scarlet" (Bathsheba too, we recall, was first seen in a crimson jacket); he radiates sexual energy. Her gasped "Oh!", in response to his "I am a man", signals the stirring in her of desire.

The reader, unlike Bathsheba, has met Troy before, first as a disembodied voice from behind a barracks wall, in a series of offhand answers to the pleading Fanny Robin; and then in Chapter 16, when Fanny mistakes the church where the marriage was to take place. His silent rigidity as he waits, the giggling of the watching women, and the "malicious leer" of the jack which strikes the quarter-hours on the church clock, are oddly discordant with the fluent performance that charms and bewilders the helpless Bathsheba. Chapter 25, 'The New Acquaintance Described', raises further questions about his character. He is a man "to whom memories were an incumbrance, and anticipations a superfluity"; he lives in the present, subject to the mood of the moment. Consistency of purpose, or fidelity for its own sake, are of no interest to him. His misogynistic advice is that women should be treated with either flattery – his tactic with Bathsheba – or cursing: "Treat them fairly, and you are a lost man." The chapter makes no reference to Fanny; it is left for the reader to ask which method he employed with her, and whether she is now present in his mind even as an "incumbrance".

The narrator is ambivalent here: the moral judgement is implied but not forced home, the sexual glamour not wholly stripped away. Pressed by Bathsheba, Liddy describes Troy as a "gay man", in the Victorian sense of that term: careless rather than vicious, more a cad than a villain. In additions made at proof stage, Hardy underlined his rootlessness by providing him with the "slight romance" of an aristocratic pedigree; as the illegitimate child of Lord Severn he is, as Fanny tells Oak, a "nobleman by blood". Like many of his contemporaries, Hardy was fascinated by the relation between ancestry, conduct and character, but having given Troy a romantic background he seems unsure how much weight to attach to it. It helps to explain (though not to justify) the instability of his nature and his easy assumption of superiority; but, as Rosemarie Morgan points out in her study of the manuscript, the increased emphasis on the social distance between him and the ever-trusting Fanny makes her appear still more vulnerable, and his treatment of her all the more heartless.

The scene in which Troy helps Bathsheba brush the bees into the hive is similarly open to alternative readings (27). On the one hand, he seems assured enough of his masculinity to wear her woman's hat and veil, reducing Bathsheba to helpless laughter (and thereby further breaking down her reserve); on the other, the episode is a prelude to the hypermasculinity of the following chapter, 'The Hollow amid the Ferns'. What becomes clear is that for Troy to act effectively, he must assume complete control; he exists in and through his effect on an audience. He begins the sword display with "a preliminary test", to ensure that Bathsheba will stand without flinching; he can "perform" only if she is motionless. Unlike Boldwood's, his power depends less on the male gaze, directed at the woman, than on ensuring that her gaze is concentrated solely on him.

That attention once granted, however, the spectacle he creates is brilliant. The setting is perfectly chosen: the concealed hollow, the "soft, feathery arms" of the ferns "caressing her up to her shoulders", the "yielding" floor of moss and grass, speak clearly of Bathsheba's unconfessed desires. As Troy "thrusts" at her, his sword "like a living thing", she finds herself "enclosed in a firmament of light, and of sharp hisses, resembling a sky-full of meteors close at hand". The erotic charge is unmissable, and unprecedented; the passage is a long orgasmic swoon. In the architecture of the novel – the echoes and parallels which shape what Lawrence calls its "metaphysic", ensuring the reader draws the "right" conclusions – the "marvellous evolutions of Troy's reflecting blade" evoke both the earlier image of Gabriel astride the rick, "whizzing his great long arms about like a windmill" as he beats off burning particles with his crook, and the later one of his battle against the storm, while the lightning flashes around him in "a perfect dance of death".

In the contrast, Oak wins out morally: he acts without regard for himself, and he is in real danger, whereas here it is Bathsheba who is put at risk. In the moment of reading, however, what we register is the magnetism of Troy's phallic display, and Bathsheba's utter submission. It is essential that we allow this its full force; to interpret his performance as *merely* theatrical, and her response as simply foolish or masochistic, is to ignore what Robert Polhemus calls "the soul-shaking power of the erotic" – a phrase that resonates with a good deal of Hardy's fiction. John Bayley describes the chapter, with some justice, as "one of the greatest scenes in English fiction".

Bathsheba, however, in half-hearted

recognition of Troy's evident faults, determines to renounce him. That decision is overthrown by the news that she has a rival. In Hardy's fiction, obstacles to desire – distance, class boundaries, the presence of another lover – almost invariably serve to increase it; just as surely, conquest or marriage cause it to diminish. In the event, Troy proves as poor a husband as Oak and the reader, and indeed Bathsheba, have expected; he gambles with his wife's money, fails to secure the ricks against the storm, and celebrates his wedding with an all-male drinking session in which the "cockbirds" are ordered to carouse while the women are sent to bed (38). Dissimilar as they are in almost every respect, neither Troy nor Boldwood can accept Bathsheba as an independent woman, not only capable of running a farm but wanting to do so.

Even so, it is unexpected that on her return to Weatherbury as a newly (albeit still secretly) married woman Bathsheba already speaks "listlessly" and seems "weary" (39). Her lassitude hints at more complex reasons for the failure of the marriage. Troy's complaint that she has become "chicken-hearted", without her former "pluck and sauciness", is prompted by his need to beg money from her, but perhaps suggests a wider disappointment: that she has not been fully responsive sexually. If so, that might be in part because he is, after all, encumbered by memories; he carries a lock of Fanny's hair, and the meeting with her on the Casterbridge highway reveals that after their attempted wedding he searched for her without success – information as new to the reader (supposing we believe it) as it is to Bathsheba. Equally important, however, is Bathsheba's pride in the "simplicity of a maiden existence": "it had been a glory to her to know that her lips had been touched by no man's on earth – that her waist had never been encircled by a lover's arm. She hated herself now" (41). Far from wanting to be tamed, as she once told Gabriel, she rages like a "caged leopard".

"Diana was the goddess whom Bathsheba instinctively adored." This sounds like an authoritative judgement, but the novel leaves it an open question how far Bathsheba's sense that marriage is a form of "spoliation" is indeed "instinctive", and how far a response to some inadequacy within Troy. She looks back longingly to the time when she felt "sufficient to herself", much as Farmer Boldwood remembers a time before he knew her, when he was content with his own "impassibleness". At one point she recognises Boldwood as "nearly her own self rendered into another sex" (31), and of her as of him it might be said that desire forces her to live "outside [her] defences". Both have supposed themselves invulnerable to sexual feeling, and are stunned when it arrives.

The similarity between them is doubly

significant. First, Hardy takes for granted something that most Victorian commentators refused even to consider: that sexual life – "the strongest passion known to humanity", as he puts it elsewhere – is as urgent and compelling for women as for men. Second, the concern for their own independence leads both Boldwood and Bathsheba to view sexual arousal as an existential threat. Precisely because Hardy admits the overwhelming power of sexual desire, he also understands why both men and women might retreat from it, fleeing, in Lawrence's terms, from engagement with the other into the "walled citadel" of their conventional selves. If Troy and Bathsheba are each left unsatisfied, the reason

## THE DOCTRINE OF THE "UNKNOWABLE"

Hardy stated that he had been influenced by the philosophy of Herbert Spencer (1820–1903), and in particular shared his belief that lying beyond whatever is known there will always be the next 'Unknowable'. In his *Literary Notebooks* Hardy transcribed part of the final paragraph of Spencer's *An Autobiography*, which reflects on what Spencer calls "a paralyzing thought": "what if, of all that is thus incomprehensible to us, there exists no comprehension anywhere? No wonder that men take refuge in authoritative dogma!" Hardy, a committed agnostic, was determined not to take any such refuge ∎

may lie in her wish for self-sufficiency, as well as in his shallowness.

The collapse of their marriage takes place beside Fanny's open coffin. Daleski writes that Troy acts here "with complete sincerity and spontaneity", and the text certainly allows such a reading: his features express "illimitable sadness", and he kisses Fanny's corpse with "an indefinable union of reverence and remorse" (43). But Troy's abandonment to his feelings is not quite the same as sincerity. Like all Hardy's lovers, Troy's passion is intensified by distance. As J. Hillis Miller has observed, because "death puts an infinite distance between lover and beloved", it "raises love to a measureless intensity". It is only when she is dead and inaccessible that Troy addresses Fanny as his "true wife".

Her death brings him no new self-knowledge. There remains the same element of cruelty that he showed Fanny when he rounds on the agonised Bathsheba: "This woman is more to me, dead as she is, than ever you were, or are, or can be... You are nothing to me – nothing." Even as he calls himself a "bad, black-hearted man", he blames Bathsheba for tempting him with her beauty and her "cursed coquetries". Both the anger and remorse are real, but they are also the fitful reflexes of a habitually insincere man. He orders Fanny's tombstone with the impatience of "a child in a nursery", and when the rain from the gargoyle washes away the flowers he had planted on her grave, he gives up:

> *He did not attempt to fill up the hole, replace the flowers, or do anything at all. He simply threw up his cards and forswore his game for that time and always. (46)*

From this point on, what sympathy the narrator has shown him is largely withdrawn. It is not only grief at Fanny's death that drives him away, but "the humdrum tediousness of a farmer's life" (47). His reappearance at Greenhill fair, in the double disguise of a circus rider playing the part of Dick Turpin, mockingly underscores his status as a performer. Ironically, he is not even the star of the show; that distinction goes to the horse, Black Bess, for ever "enshrined" in the memories of the audience. He is forced into a shabby alliance with Pennyways, the bailiff dismissed for theft, who identifies him beneath his make-up. His decision to reclaim Bathsheba is not made for love, though seeing her with Boldwood prompts a moment's jealousy, but because she has money, a house and a farm.

The scene of his arrival at Boldwood's Christmas party (53) is deliberately melodramatic: he laughs "a mechanical laugh", and speaks to Bathsheba in the tones of a stage villain: "Come, madam, do you hear what I say?" For a moment she remains motionless, in a state of "mental *gutta serena*", blind to all about her: as John Lucas comments, she "literally cannot see Troy because since he is no longer a vision to her he is nothing. He has ceased to have an identity which she can acknowledge." She reacts with "a quick, low scream" only when he seizes her arm.

With Troy's death, and Bathsheba's reaction to it, the mood shifts to one of pathos. She washes and prepares his body, rather than letting his corpse "bide neglected for folks to stare at" (54), before she herself sinks in "a shapeless heap of drapery" – two more examples in this novel of the vulnerable human body. He is buried alongside Fanny, with an inscription that reminds the reader that he died young, "aged 26 years". The chapter which includes that information (56) begins "Bathsheba revived with the spring." The novel recovers the form of pastoral: Troy's death and Boldwood's incarceration, deep in the midwinter, make room for a spirit of renewal.

That is not, however, quite the end of the matter. Those who read the novel as a story about the chastening of a wilful woman may feel that Bathsheba's unruly longings have been buried with her first husband, and her marriage to Gabriel is a simple gain. Yet it is difficult to imagine that her second husband will "set her stinging as if aflame to the very hollows of her feet"; Oak and Troy are not the same "sort of man". In choosing "*camaraderie*" with Oak – companionate rather than ecstatic love – Bathsheba risks surrendering the part of her nature expressed in her desire for Troy. The relation between passion and constancy is a subject Hardy would return to in later novels and in many of his finest poems. In 1926, in his mid-eighties, he noted approvingly Proust's bleak summary of sexual love: *"Le désir s'élève, se satisfait, disparaît – et c'est tout"*: desire stirs, is satisfied, disappears – and that is all. But as *Far from the Madding Crowd* reveals, it is not all Hardy had to say.

# What is Hardy's attitude towards women in *Far from the Madding Crowd*?

However lovable and charming Bathsheba may be, still she is weak; however stubborn and ill-guided Henchard may be, still he is strong. This is fundamental; this is the core of Hardy's vision, and draws from the deepest sources of his nature. The woman is the weaker and the fleshlier, and she clings to the stronger and obscures his vision.

— Virginia Woolf

In Chapter 30 of *Far from the Madding Crowd* Bathsheba asks Liddy in some alarm whether she appears "a bold sort of maid – mannish?" Liddy replies, reassuringly, "Oh no, not mannish; but so almighty womanish that 'tis getting on that way sometimes." The question of what constituted "womanish" or "womanly" behaviour and character dominated the period in which Hardy was writing, and as a novelist dealing with love and courtship it was one he could hardly avoid, but what his own position might have been, particularly in the early part of his career, is not easily decided. Rosemarie Morgan sees him as the champion of women's moral, intellectual and especially sexual independence, and explains the occasional narratorial asides about women's "vanity" or "weakness" as a ruse to deflect the suspicions of his more conservative readers.

Patricia Ingham suggests that he "struggles but fails to accept a patriarchal view", with inconsistencies in the novels revealing ideological "faultlines" in Victorian sexual politics. Roger Ebbatson writes of "the creative uncertainties of Hardy's handling of gender issues", a phrase nicely neutral as to whether he is to be seen as diagnosing the contradictions in his society's attitudes, or as merely symptomatic of them.

The range of views is understandable. What the Victorian press referred to as "the woman question" was on one level a debate about the laws governing marriage, divorce and child custody, the double standard of sexual morality (chastity for women, licence for men), women's access to higher education and the professions, and the right of women to own property or to vote. Hardy's fiction engages with all but the last of these, and in each case on what the 21st century reader might consider the more progressive side.

But critical and urgent as these issues were, the more profound dispute was about the meaning to be attached to the signifier "woman". Mainstream opinion in Victorian England held that the natures of men and (especially) of women were fixed and given, the one active, rational, and intended for rule, the other passive, intuitive, and designed to serve. To men of the Church these differences had been ordained by God, to the men of science they had been biologically determined in the process of evolution, but both sides were agreed that these were fundamental divisions, properly reflected in the existing structures of society, in which men engaged in the open world, and women were confined to the home. As John Ruskin wrote, eloquently but complacently, "a true wife, in her husband's house, is his servant", but "in his heart... she is queen". The woman who argued otherwise was not "true".

From around the mid-century, however, an increasing number of women challenged this position on the basis of their own experience. Why, demanded Florence Nightingale, do women, no less than men, have "passion, intellect, moral activity", yet a place in society where no one of the three could be exercised? John Stuart Mill, one of the thinkers Hardy most admired, went further, arguing in *The Subjection of Women* (1869) that the very concept of "woman's nature" was a false one: what was called "the nature of women" was in reality "an eminently artificial thing – the result of forced repression in some directions, unnatural stimulation in others". The assumed divisions between men and women were not based on some reality in "nature", but socially constructed; the site of women's disabilities was not their inherent weakness, but the organisation of society, and that at least was open to change.

LESLIE STEPHEN,
HARDY'S FIRST
EDITOR

Hardy gives a teasing account of his contact with Stephen in his autobiography. First, he suggests that postal arrangements in his native Dorset were "so primitive" that one of Stephen's letters was handed to him by a labourer who had picked it up from a muddy lane, where it had been dropped by the schoolchildren asked to deliver it.

Second, he claims that he worked on the novel in the intervals of helping with the cider-making, "sometimes indoors, sometimes out", and

Hardy's later work is open and often angry in its opposition to the sexual double standard (*Tess*), the deliberate inequities in the laws governing marriage and divorce (*The Woodlanders, Jude*), and the economic disadvantages suffered by women (*The Woodlanders, Tess*). He told the suffragist Millicent Fawcett that he supported giving women the vote because it would help

> break up the present pernicious conventions in respect of manners, customs, religion, illegitimacy, the stereotyped household (that it must be the unit of society), the father of a woman's child (that it is anybody's business but the woman's own) as well as bring about an end to blood sports and cruelty to animals.

occasionally finding himself without paper to write on "would use large dead leaves, white chips left by the wood-cutters, or pieces of stone or slate that came to hand".

Numerous readers have been happy to take all this on trust, presumably without trying the experiment of writing on leaves, let alone with chips of wood. But Hardy was surely being ironical. Leslie Stephen, Cambridge-educated and Bloomsbury to the core, the future editor of the *Dictionary of National Biography* (and father of Virginia Woolf), was to become a friend, and in their religious and scientific beliefs the two had much in common. But Stephen also represented the literary establishment which found it so difficult to deal with what the Oxford-educated Matthew Arnold called "provincial" writing and writers – which meant, in

This was too radical for Fawcett, who wisely decided not to use his letter in her campaign. But his stance is less clear-cut in the earlier fiction, including *Far from the Madding Crowd*, where the narrator's comments about women are typically essentialist, and often misogynistic: "Women's prescriptive infirmity [vanity] had stalked into the sunlight..." (1); "that novelty among women – one who finished a thought before beginning the sentence which conveyed it" (3); "In arguing on prices she held to her own firmly... and reduced theirs persistently, as was inevitable in a woman" (12); "Women are never tired of bewailing man's fickleness in love, but they seem only to snub his

effect, all those not educated at one of the ancient universities. The silliest version of this position belongs to the novelist and playwright W. Somerset Maugham (educated at Heidelberg), who thought that even in formal evening dress Hardy "had still a strange look of the soil". Hardy had nothing to do with "the soil"; his father was a master mason, not a farmer, and he himself spent 16 years working with some success as an architect, restoring churches and designing board schools. Critics and biographers have at times written patronisingly about him, but Hardy read as widely, and with as much insight, as the great majority of his contemporaries. If he is sometimes described as "self-educated", the best reply remains: what other sort of education is there?

Leslie Stephen, certainly, respected Hardy enough to ask him rather than one of his Bloomsbury friends to

*Leslie Stephen with his wife Julia and daughter Virgina, 1893. There is a chance that Vanessa Stephen (later Vanessa Bell) took this photograph of her sister (later Virginia Woolf) and their parents during summer holidays at Talland House, St. Ives.*

witness his renunciation of Holy Orders in 1875, when the two talked together about theology, "the constitution of matter, the unreality of time, and kindred subjects".

Hardy in his turn trusted the older man's editorial advice, at least at the outset of his career, when his chief ambition was to be considered a "good hand at a serial"; Stephen understood magazine audiences better than Hardy did, and many of his deletions can be defended on the grounds that they help maintain tension in the novel.

But though an intellectual and free-thinker, Stephen was uncomfortable with Hardy's frankness about sexual matters, and in 1877 he refused to make an offer for *The Return of the Native* unless he could see and approve the complete manuscript in advance. Hardy decided instead to publish elsewhere, and sent him no more of his work. Even so, the two remained on good terms until Stephen's death in 1904 ∎

constancy" (24); and so on. Whatever Thomas Hardy may have thought, his narrator seems willing to recycle conservative views of women as the weaker vessels.

But the contrary case is present as well. The narrator remarks on Bathsheba's "impulsive" nature, but in a novel in which Troy abandons two women, Boldwood commits murder, and even the "steady" Oak comes close to death through his own carelessness, dismissive aphorisms about women's folly will hardly impress the reader. More fundamentally, Bathsheba struggles to assert a degree of agency that the men in the novel are reluctant to concede. Bullied and interrogated by

HARDY'S RUSTICS

In a letter to Leslie Stephen about the illustrations to *Far from the Madding Crowd*, Hardy hoped that "the rustics, although quaint, may be made to appear intelligent, and not boorish at all". The same concern underlies his handling of dialect in the novel: on the one hand, he aimed to record the richness, vitality and "quaintness" of the Dorset dialect; on the other, he wanted to show his rustic characters (as one reviewer put it) as "shrewd, racy, and wise" and possessing "considerable powers of thought".

Hardy's attitude to the Dorset dialect was shaped by his family life. His father used dialect forms uninhibitedly; his mother, ambitious for her

Boldwood, as Elfride is by Henry Knight in *A Pair of Blue Eyes*, and as Eustacia, Tess and Sue will be in later novels, Bathsheba makes the protest that they too might have made: "It is difficult for a woman to define her feelings in language which is chiefly made by men to express theirs" (51). One after another Hardy's heroines are asked to explain themselves in "men's language", and find themselves unable to do so; the texts open up on a discrepancy between the way they perceive themselves and the way they are perceived by others. If in the end they are worn down by the demand to justify what are presented to them as their errors, that is less a comment on their

children, worked hard to adopt standard speech – dialect, Hardy wrote, was "not spoken in his mother's house". Tess Durbeyfield speaks "two languages; the dialect at home, more or less; ordinary English abroad and to persons of quality".

So too, presumably, did the young Hardy, at least until he went to school in Dorchester. However firmly he agreed with his friend, the poet and philologist William Barnes, that Dorset dialect was not "a corruption of correct English" but "a distinct branch of Teutonic speech", he quickly learned that its use was seen by others as a marker of class as well as regional origins.

The many changes to rustic speech over the various editions of *Far from the Madding Crowd* show Hardy exploring what readers would accept. Of the leading characters, only Gabriel uses dialect forms (though even the town-bred Bathsheba occasionally uses *'tis* and *'twould* for *it is* and *it would*). As one might expect of a man trying to improve himself,

weakness than a recognition of the forces lined up against them.

In his preface to the 1896 edition of *The Woodlanders*, Hardy remarked that in this story, "as in one or two others in this series which involve the question of matrimonial divergence, the immortal puzzle – given the man and the woman, how to find a basis for their sexual relation – is left where it stood".

Hardy liked to attach such disclaimers to his work, and his readers, then and since, have generally ignored them. In *Far from the Madding*

however, Gabriel uses them inconsistently: in Warren's malthouse, among the workfolk, he asks "what sort of a mis'ess" Bathsheba is to work for, but to her he uses the standard form "mistress".

Elsewhere he uses "tined" rather than closed, "mind" for remember, "afeard" for afraid, "stepped ath'art" for came over, and so on. Only occasionally does he employ the most vivid dialect forms, as when warning Mark Clark not to use his "smack-and-coddle style" (kiss and cuddle) when speaking of Bathsheba. But even in the closing pages of the novel, the linguistic gap between him and Bathsheba is not fully closed; his speech remains somewhere between hers and that of the workfolk (or "souls", as Oak greets them) who come to celebrate their wedding.

With the other characters, Hardy allows himself more freedom with dialect words: "plimmed" for inflated, "snap" for snack, "thirtover" for perverse, "limber" for frail, etc. When Bathsheba asks about the cause of Fanny's death, Joseph Poorgrass attributes it in the manuscript to "inflammation of the lungs", amended to "a

*Crowd* the question is left unanswered, but hardly "where it stood". The subject of the novel is not quite, as Henry James and others have supposed, the chastening and education of Bathsheba Everdene, so much as the attempt of three men to impose on her their own name, and their idea of who and what she should be: to remake her as Bathsheba Troy, or Bathsheba Boldwood, or Bathsheba Oak. In the process, as this guide has suggested, what counts as "manly" comes under question as much as what is "womanly". What the reader who inclines to James's view might regard

general weakness of constitution". In the printed text this becomes "a general neshness of constitution", with Hardy trusting the reader to interpret the unfamiliar term. At the same time, he amended Joseph's "She was soon gone, it seems" to "'a went like a candle-snoff, so 'tis said" (i.e. like a snuffed candle), and "She was taken ill" to "She was took bad." The rather moving effect is to reintegrate Fanny, the lost woman, into the local community.

Hardy necessarily accommodated himself, and his texts, to the expectations of a metropolitan audience, but he continued to find ways of challenging the Victorian stereotype of the rustic boor known and patronised under the generic name of "Hodge". One of his Wessex characters, now living in London, might be allowed the last word: "If I talk the Wessex way 'tisn't for want of knowing better; 'tis because my staunch nater makes me bide faithful to our old ancient institutions" (*The Hand of Ethelberta*). The "Wessex way" was under threat, not least from increased and better schooling, but it had - and deserved - its defenders ∎

# TEN FACTS ABOUT
## *FAR FROM THE MADDING CROWD*

### 1.

In September 1874, a couple of months after completing work on *Far from the Madding Crowd*, Hardy married Emma Gifford, entering his profession as "Author" in the marriage register. He and Emma had met in Cornwall in 1870, when Hardy was still an architect.

### 2.

Bathsheba shares some of Emma's enthusiasms, notably horse riding, something Hardy never mastered. Her acrobatic feat of dropping "backwards flat upon the pony's back, her head over its tail, her feet against its shoulders and her eyes to the sky" prompts the question, says Claire Tomalin, of whether Hardy ever saw Emma ride this way, without her habit and side saddle.

### 3.

In 1906 Hardy wrote that "but for a stupid blunder of God almighty" he might have married Helen Paterson, who illustrated *Far from the Madding Crowd* for the *Cornhill*. In fact, Paterson also got married in 1874, to the poet and diarist William Allingham; the November and December illustrations bear the signature 'H. Allingham', rather than "H. Paterson" or "H.P.". Hardy's poem "The Opportunity (For H.P.)" reflects on what he at least thought a missed chance; there is no record of what the then Miss Paterson thought of him.

## 4.

Hardy first saw his novel in print when he bought a copy of the *Cornhill* at the railway station in Plymouth, on his way to see Emma. He was surprised to find it had been given pride of place. As often in serial fiction, the illustration came before the event it portrayed: in this case, the opening vignette for the letter W ("When Farmer Oak smiled...") is of a young woman (Bathsheba) carrying a heavy pail, while the plate on the first page shows her saving Oak from suffocation in his hut, above the caption "Hands Were Loosening His Neckerchief".

## 5.

*Far from the Madding Crowd* has been adapted for film and television at least four times. The first was a silent version, released in 1915. The John Schlesinger film of 1967, starring Julie Christie, Alan Bates (Oak), Terence Stamp (Troy) and Peter Finch (Boldwood) was shot entirely within the boundaries of Hardy's Wessex, unlike the Granada TV version (1998), which is set in the north of England. David Nicholls is the latest to write a screenplay from the novel, the film directed by Thomas Vinterberg and starring Carey Mulligan alongside Michael Sheen (2014).

## 6.
Hardy prepared a stage version of the novel, with the title *The Mistress of the Farm: A Pastoral Drama*, in collaboration with J. Comyns Carr. The project was put aside, but the actress Madge Kendal recounted the plot to the dramatist Arthur Wing Pinero, who made it the basis of his own play *The Squire* (1881). Hardy wrote complaining to *The Times*, Pinero replied in the *Daily News*, and Comyns Carr took the chance offered by the publicity to revise *The Mistress of the Farm*, now called *Far from the Madding Crowd*. It opened in 1882. It was the first of a long series of stage and film adaptations of Hardy's fiction.

## 7.
Hardy tells us that much of *Far from the Madding Crowd* was written out of doors, on scraps of slate or stone, pieces of wood and even dead leaves – which, says Claire Tomalin in her biography, is "hard to believe – how much can you write on a dead leaf? – but absurdly appropriate to the rural setting of the book, and the storm scene was actually written during a night of thunder and lightning".

## 8.

Hardy was paid £400 for the serial and first volume publication of *Far from the Madding Crowd* (approx. £40,000 in today's money). There were further earnings from the US edition, the later one-volume edition, translations, etc. By contrast, two years earlier he had sold the copyright for *Under the Greenwood Tree* for a mere £30; after a temporary fall in popularity in the early 1880s, his 10th novel, *The Mayor of Casterbridge* (1886) earned him £200.

## 9.

Weatherbury is Hardy's name for Puddletown in Dorset, the name coming from the original spelling of Weatherby Castle, an Iron Age hill fort at nearby Milborne St Andrew. Puddletown was a small but busy market town in the middle of the 19th century, and the one nearest to Hardy's birthplace at Bockhampton. Its correct name was Piddletown; Puddletown was a polite Victorian emendation.

## 10.

Much of the description of Bathsheba's house and the 14th and 15th century church at Weatherbury is closely based on fact, though some distances have been slightly altered. The hideous gargoyles which hurl water onto Fanny's grave, however, were borrowed from elsewhere.

*Poster for the 1915 silent film, the first film to be made from the novel*

as Bathsheba's fickleness in being unable to choose between the men who court her may better be seen as the novelist's recognition that no one of the three is great enough to subsume her identity within their own. Like any other writer, even the most iconoclastic, Hardy could never wholly free himself from the weight of received assumptions, including those about "woman"; but throughout his fiction he upheld the complex right of all individuals, men and women alike, to be themselves. He is less concerned with the supposedly given fact of "woman's nature", than the way in which Bathsheba's right to be herself comes into conflict with the ideology of womanhood.

Contrary to Virginia Woolf's words, quoted earlier, Bathsheba does not "obscure" the man's vision. Rather, men's language, and men's way of seeing, begin to obscure our vision of her. The rustics make fun, on the last page of the novel, of Oak's newly acquired facility in speaking of "my wife", and it would be reading against the grain to make too much of their comments; Oak will make a decent husband, and the conclusion is not without its promise of happiness. Even so, the sympathetic reader will put the book down reflecting that Bathsheba is more than the sum of those two words.

## How much does Fanny suffer?

In Chapter 43, as Bathsheba watches Troy bend over Fanny's coffin, the narrator risks the thought that since "Capacity for intense feeling is proportionate to the general intensity of the nature", Fanny may never have "suffered in an absolute sense what Bathsheba suffered now". The idea seems plausible when applied across species – as for example to the emotional hurt felt by human beings and the physical pain experienced by ants or flies – but used to contrast one human being with another it is, as Hardy was aware, a dangerous argument, much favoured in the 1850s and 1860s by those who wished to defend slavery abroad or class privilege at home. In Dickens's *David Copperfield*, the spiteful Rosa Dartle asks whether the poor and simple are

> really animals and clods, and beings of another order... It's such a delight to know that, when they suffer, they don't feel!

For a writer like Hardy, whose rustic characters were dismissed in the London *Athenaeum* as "illiterate clods", as for Wordsworth and George

## FOLLOWING THE SEASONS

The publication of *Far from the Madding Crowd* in 12 monthly instalments allowed Hardy to link the events of the farming year to the calendar month of publication. Thus the opening chapters, featuring Gabriel's midwinter work with his flock, appeared in January, the February instalment opened with "a day in February", and Chapters 9–14, including the sending of the Valentine and its aftermath, came out in March. Lambing time was described in the April issue, the sheep-shearing scenes in May, the hiving of the bees in

Eliot before him, the idea that sensitivity to pain was relative to intelligence or social status was necessarily troubling: how could the suffering of the inarticulate poor – the so-called "beings of another order" – be registered in a way that would engage the middle-class reader? The story of Fanny Robin is in part Hardy's attempt to answer that question.

Fanny's role as a fallen woman troubled Hardy's conservative editor Leslie Stephen, but as Linda Shires has observed she is also

> the problem of the book...[Hardy] will retell a story like hers in *Tess of the d'Urbervilles* where he takes the entire novel to do it justice.

June. The great summer storm "at the end of August" appeared in the August issue.

The instalments recounting Fanny's death, the journey of her coffin to Weatherbury through the autumn fog, and Troy's departure, came out in September and October.

The November issue covered the whole period of Troy's absence, which begins in the October of one year and ends shortly before Christmas in the next.

The final issue, centred on Boldwood's Christmas Eve party, appeared in December.

In tracking the farming year, Hardy was consciously evoking earlier English pastoral writing, such as Spenser's *Shepheardes Calender* (1579); more subversively, he was also reminding his largely urban audience of the distance, morally and spatially, between rural and metropolitan life and ways ∎

She is first met, but not named, in Chapter 7, "thinly clad", and half-concealed outside the churchyard wall – her choice of position perhaps a hint of her fallen status – where she is described simply as "a figure", a "motionless stranger", "a slim girl", and then a "young woman": a mere portion of humanity rather than an individual. When Gabriel touches her wrist in handing her a shilling, it beats with "a throb of tragic intensity", which is at the same time like the beat in "the femoral artery of his lambs when overdriven". Her plight has taken her to the point where human tragedy borders on simple animal vulnerability.

As he moves on, Gabriel senses that he had been "in the penumbra of a very deep sadness when touching that slight and fragile creature". The word "creature", as Anna West has well shown, was charged with meaning for Hardy; in this novel alone he uses it 17 times, to describe lambs, chain salpae (a marine organism), a toad and a stray dog, as well as both Boldwood and Bathsheba. When Parson Thirdly speaks of Fanny after her death as a "fellow-creature", the phrase embodies Hardy's Darwinian belief in the deep kinship of human and non-human animals – their shared creatureliness – at least as much as orthodox Christian teaching.

Fanny's marginal status is emphasised again in the scene outside Troy's barracks (11). She is at first merely "a form" by the brink of the river, "small", visible only in "outline", though "it seemed human". By the time she attracts Troy's attention, she is "a blurred spot in the snow". When he asks, "What girl are you?" she answers, part truthfully, partly in hope, "Your wife, Fanny Robin," but as she retreats back into the night she is again a "little spot": not legally a wife, but the fallen woman, whose history Victorian society wished to leave "blurred", or at least censored, in life as in fiction. Significantly, Fanny is the subject of only one of Helen Allingham's full-page illustrations in the *Cornhill* serial version of the novel; it shows her the night before her death in childbirth, but so positioned that her pregnancy is wholly hidden.

In the three subsequent scenes in which Fanny appears – on what should have been her wedding day, the meeting with Troy and Bathsheba on the Casterbridge highway, and her final journey to the Union workhouse – she is again left unnamed by the narrator. In the first of these she is a "little woman" (39), whose expression of anxiety changes to one of "terror" when she sees Troy's anger; in the second, a "woman", who utters a "hysterical cry" before she collapses. This proves the moment which might have saved her life; Bathsheba exclaims "Oh, poor thing!" and is about to go to her help until forbidden by Troy, more concerned with his own position than the woman who is carrying his child.

Bathsheba and Troy drive on, the latter giving

"a smart cut of the whip" to the horse. The reader and narrator remain with Fanny, who becomes the eternal fallen woman in her hopeless anonymity: "the crouching woman", "the pedestrian", "the wayfarer", "a shapeless heap", and finally a "prostrate figure". The only recognition of her plight comes not from another human being, but a dog; as she becomes weaker, and loses her sense of purpose, the dog "thoroughly" understands her incapacity, and becomes "frantic in his distress" on her account, tugging at her clothing to urge her on (40).

That the dog is of no identifiable breed – like Fanny, it too is described as a "creature" – allows the chapter to be read as a virtual test case for Darwin's speculation in *The Descent of Man* (1871) that some of the "higher" animals, such as dogs, might already have evolved "something very like a

## AN EYE FOR COLOUR

To an extent unmatched even in Emily Brontë's *Wuthering Heights* or George Eliot's *Adam Bede*, the daily lives of Hardy's men and women are shaped by their physical environment – the weather, the time of day, and above all the light.

In *Far from the Madding Crowd*, more than half the action takes place in darkness, variously lit by the moon, stars, lanterns, fire or flashes of lightning. Like

conscience" – rather more of one, in this instance, than the man who claims to have loved her. In a bitter irony, Fanny is admitted into the workhouse (the first time in the novel that she has been sheltered from the elements), but the dog is "stoned... away". Victorian society had learned from Christ's example in the Gospel of St John (Chapter 8) not to stone an adulterous woman, but the impulse to "cast the first stone" remained.

Fanny's claim to individual personhood has been so slight that death hardly seems to diminish it. Poorgrass becomes too drunk to drive home her coffin; Gabriel rubs the words "and child" from the coffin lid. Her story is subsumed within the apparently greater one of Bathsheba's marriage; when Bathsheba opens the coffin it is to find "conclusive proof of her husband's conduct", not to learn more of Fanny (43). The discovery of the

Turner, whose paintings he studied and admired, Hardy is fascinated by moments when the light is changing, like the "slow sunrise" to which Boldwood awakes in Chapter 14; the sun shining on his white hearthstone "like a red and flameless fire"; the "slow twilight" at the shearing-supper, as the sun sets "in an ochreous mist"; or the "monotonous pallor" of the autumn fog that descends on Poorgrass as he journeys back from the workhouse with Fanny's coffin. The volatility of the atmosphere acts as a reminder that we all inhabit a world of change, and change with it.

The effects of darkness, sunshine and the various kinds of half-light make themselves felt in the characters' moods and

baby leaves her at first angry at her dead rival, then tempted to match her by dying herself; only later – implicitly identifying with her as a betrayed woman – does she try to make "atonement" by surrounding her with flowers, as if preparing her bridal bed. Troy embraces Fanny as his "very wife", regardless of her legal status, but within 48 hours has left the area; when he returns, it is to reclaim Bathsheba as his wife, and her home and money as legally his.

Fanny's story can be compared with that of Hetty Sorrel in George Eliot's *Adam Bede* (1859). In both novels, the fallen, pregnant woman makes a long and arduous journey; in both, contrary to Victorian fictional conventions, their travails bring no illumination or redemption; both women die. Yet Hetty is guilty of killing her child, and her death can be seen as a judgement; Fanny is wholly

---

decisions. Bathsheba and Troy first meet on a path "black as the ninth plague of Egypt at midnight". Troy is "brilliant in brass and scarlet", his appearance as dramatic as the sound of a trumpet breaking the silence; the light from Bathsheba's lantern radiates upwards, throwing "gigantic shadows" which become "distorted and mangled" on the tree trunks. The sword exercise takes place just before sunset on a summer evening, "whilst the bristling ball of gold in the west still swept the tips of the ferns with its long, luxuriant rays".

The following chapter, as Bathsheba drifts towards the recognition that she is falling in love, is titled 'Particulars of

innocent, and her death is felt as a rebuke to the world which could find no place for her. Hardy did not consider himself a preacher, but there is a clear protest here on behalf of all those who are pushed beyond the margins of society, treated as "beings of another order" rather than "fellow-creatures". He made the point in an interview in later life:

> What are my works but one plea against "man's inhumanity to man" – and to woman – and to the lower animals?

a Twilight Walk'. This is closer to a poetics (or an erotics) of light than simple scene-setting. Throughout the novel, Hardy's eye for colour is at once exact and startling: the moon is "chrome-yellow" on the night Gabriel loses his sheep, like "tarnished brass" as Boldwood ponders the valentine, "lurid" and "metallic" the night before the storm, "pale primrose" as Bathsheba makes her way to Gabriel's cottage to see if he will stay. The range and brilliance of Hardy's palette invokes and corresponds to the irruptions of feeling in the lives of his heroes and heroines. Literally, they are forced to see the world, and themselves, in a new light ∎

# What is the role of Nature in *Far from the Madding Crowd*?

 "The very ground-thought of Science," Hardy copied into his notebook, "is to treat man as part of the natural order." The concept of Nature, or the natural order – what it "meant", if indeed it had any meaning, and where humanity fitted into it – underwent profound changes during the 19th century. At its outset, the physical world was widely seen as God's "second book", testimony to the power, wisdom and goodness of the Creator; by its end, developments in geology had introduced what we now know as "deep time", astronomers had begun investigating deep space, and Darwin had proposed the theory of evolution by natural selection.

For the most part Victorian science interpreted Nature as an alien place, not designed for humanity, nor in any comforting sense designed at all. This was the world-view described by Max Weber as "the disenchantment of the world": the vision of a morally indifferent universe, subject to laws operating by regular sequence, in which consciousness is the by-product of chance collocations of matter, and change the only constant. Hardy summarised in his notebooks the arguments of James Cotter Morison's

*The Service of Man*:

> Decay & death stamped not only on man & his works, but on all that surrounds him. Nature herself decays – Alps – Sun himself – from the animalcule to the galaxy.

All of Nature is subject to the same laws. There is no exemption for humanity.

"The more we know of the laws & nature of the Universe," Hardy wrote in 1902, "the more ghastly a business we perceive it all to be." The impersonal operation of natural laws, the power of chance, the inevitability of change, and the anomaly of human consciousness: seen in these terms, the universe might well be thought "ghastly". Numerous critics have emphasised Hardy's use of geological and astronomical scales to destabilise both temporal and spatial perspectives in his writing, and thereby expose the irrelevance of humanity in a boundless, uncaring universe. In his poem "Nature's Questioning" the unknown force that created the world is imaged as a "Vast Imbecility", which first framed life "in jest" and then left it to "hazardry"; in *Far from the Madding Crowd*, ricks burn, trees are blasted by lightning, sheep die in agony, Bathsheba sleeps by a poisonous swamp, Troy comes close to being drowned, and the flowers on Fanny's grave are washed away by floods of rain.

But this is clearly not all there is to say about

Hardy's representation of the natural world, and our relationship to it. Consider the opening of Chapter 27, in which Bathsheba waits to hive her bees. At first their movements are "unruly" but at last they settle:

*A process somewhat analogous to that of alleged formations of the universe, time and times ago, was observable. The bustling swarm had swept the sky in a scattered and uniform haze, which now thickened to a nebulous centre: this glided on to a bough and grew still denser, till it formed a solid black spot upon the light.*

The reference here is to the "nebular hypothesis", the subject of fascinated discussion across Victorian culture. It proposed that the universe began as an unstable swirl of dust, gradually

## THROBBING

"Throb" is one of Hardy's key words. In his novels, to be alive is to feel the movement of the blood, and the quickening of the pulse, or of the breath, and to sense it in others. It is not only the stars that throb: so too do Fanny, Bathsheba, and Boldwood.

*the twinkling of the stars seemed to be but throbs of one body, timed by a common pulse.* (2)

*She extended her hand; Gabriel his. In feeling for*

contracting into nebulae, which in turn collapsed under the force of gravity to form the stars and planets. What might have been a merely conventional piece of scene-painting prior to Bathsheba's third encounter with Troy is made to reveal an unexpected link between bees landing on an apple-tree, and the origin of the universe. Each, the small and the great, is part of 'Nature'.

So too, we can infer, are the man and woman engaged in the rituals of courtship; readers familiar with Darwin's theory of sexual selection, set out in *The Descent of Man* only three years earlier, might have noted the similarities between Troy's broadsword demonstration in the following chapter and the mating displays of stags and peacocks. But there is no suggestion that either scene diminishes Troy or Bathsheba, or invites the reader to see the feelings that move them as

*each other's palm in the gloom before the money could be passed, a minute incident occurred which told much. Gabriel's fingers alighted on the young woman's wrist. It was beating with a throb of tragic intensity.* (7)

*The swift music of her heart became hubbub now, and she throbbed to extremity.*

*He was coming to Troy. He did then know what had occurred!* (31)

*"She promises that you shall – quite natural," said the strategic lover, throbbing throughout him at the presumption which Liddy's words appeared to warrant – that his darling had thought of re-marriage.* (49) ∎

insignificant. They are simultaneously part of what Hardy calls (in *The Woodlanders*) "the great web of human doings then weaving in both hemispheres", and unique individuals faced with the conflicting pulls of love, desire, money and status.

Implicit in this discussion have been two senses of the word "Nature", which inform each other but are analytically distinct: the system or order which appears to govern the physical world (Nature with a capital N), and the various objects – rocks, plants, animals, humanity – which make up that world. In this second sense, the idea that Hardy sees humankind as part of his natural world is a virtual truism. Every reader of the novels will have noticed how much of the action takes place "in nature", or outdoors. We remember his characters along with the features of the landscapes in which we meet them – cornfields, hillsides, woodlands, pastures, heath, skyline – or the various man-made structures only one degree removed from the natural: ancient paths and barrows, hurdles thatched with straw, the malthouse, the hut in which Oak takes shelter at lambing time.

The usual distinction between indoors and out seems hardly to exist in *Far from the Madding Crowd*, where buildings and the natural world blend rather than contrast. Bathsheba's farmhouse

*Opposite: Julie Christie (Bathsheba), whom Al Pacino called "the most poetic of all actresses", in Schlesinger's 1967 film.*

is covered in "soft brown mosses, like faded velveteen"; tufts of houseleek sprout from the walls of the surrounding buildings (9). The aged maltster is in much the same condition, his white hair and beard overgrowing his figure "like the grey moss and lichen upon a leafless apple-tree" (8).

Conversely, the plantation in which Bathsheba encounters Troy resembles "a vast, low, naturally formed hall, the plumy ceiling of which was supported by slender pillars of living wood". At different times Oak, Fanny, Troy and Bathsheba all sleep beneath the stars. It is not until Chapter 56 (out of 57) that Oak and Bathsheba have their first conversation indoors, when unsurprisingly they

### HARDY'S ATTITUDE TO CHANGE

In *The Country and the City* (1973) Raymond Williams argues that "the real Hardy country" is the "border country": the border "between custom and education, between work and ideas, between love of place and an experience of change".

In Hardy's later novels, the tension between the local and the cosmopolitan, the traditional and the modern, is felt more strongly than in *Far from the Madding Crowd*, but even here he writes both as a native and celebrant of "Wessex" life and customs, and as an outsider who knows that they are under threat: such factors as increased

feel "awkward and constrained" to be sitting down together.

The most immediate result of the outdoor setting is that in Hardy's novels, almost for the first time in English fiction, characters get soaked, chilled, burned by the sun, grimy with smoke, stained or scratched by foliage. Their bodies are in constant interchange with the physical world around them; they find caterpillars on their clothes, like the one Sergeant Troy executes in 'The Hollow amid the Ferns', or look down at their boots, as Boldwood does, to see them "bronzed in artistic gradations" by pollen from the buttercups. This is of a piece with Hardy's emphasis on the fact

class mobility, education, the desire for social refinement all quietly present in the novel, and embodied in Oak and Bathsheba as much as in the obviously rootless Troy – will inevitably challenge the cohesion of the local community.

Hardy was tough-minded enough to see that this would mean gain as well as loss: it is easily overlooked that Gabriel and Bathsheba are incomers, albeit from no great distance, who introduce new skills and new ideas. In Chapter 15 the news that an old apple-tree has been uprooted prompts the maltster ("the aged man of malt") to reflect on "stirring times": "how the face of nations alter, and what we live to see nowadays!" Comic as it is in context, Hardy's Wessex fiction shows the remark to be a true one. In the course of the novel the tenancy of one farm passes to Bathsheba, the other to Oak; with their marriage the two are united, and will be differently managed. Not even Weatherbury is immune to change ■

that human beings live in bodies, and bodies live and move in the natural world: they blush, tremble, throb, quiver, flinch, pulsate, faint or stand rigid, as much as they think or reflect. Gilles Deleuze understandably suggests that his characters are not so much "people or subjects" as "collections of intensive sensations".

The second chapter of *Far from the Madding Crowd* suggests the kind of attention Hardy expects his reader to give to 'Nature'. On one level not much happens: a shepherd looks after his flock during a midwinter night on Norcombe Hill; a lamb is born; elsewhere on the hillside two women attend to a cow and a day-old calf. But the chapter is also an exuberant and many-layered meditation on a world known in time and space. The seeming

### THE TEXTS OF *FAR FROM THE MADDING CROWD*

All of Hardy's novels had a complicated publishing history. This does more than provide work for textual scholars: it also has a direct bearing on the versions of the novels that we now read. In the case of *Far from the Madding Crowd* the textual issues begin with comparison of the manuscript, now held at Yale University, and the serial version in the *Cornhill Magazine*, and the evidence this affords of numerous revisions made to meet the demands of Hardy's editor,

permanence of the hill is set against thoughts of some future day of geological "confusion", when "grander heights" and "granite precipices" will "topple". The beech plantation which covers one side is "ancient and decaying". From the north comes a "desolating" wind, together with a vocabulary which combines sound and motion: *wandered, smote, floundered, gushed, ferreting, hurrying, plunged, continued to beat*. Dead leaves *simmer* and *boil* in the ditches, *spin* across the grass, or *fall* with a *rattle* against the tree trunks.

That rattle is only one of myriad noises, as breezes of differing powers *rub, rake* or *brush* the thin grasses, while trees and hedges *moan, wail, chant* and *sob*. Above, the sky is as active as the land: the Pleiades are *restless*, Orion *soars* above

Leslie Stephen. The first hardback edition of *Far from the Madding Crowd*, in two volumes, printed essentially the same text as the *Cornhill*. Hardy made a number of changes for a cheap one-volume edition in 1877; many more for the two collected editions, the "Wessex Novels" in 1895-6, and the Macmillan "Wessex Edition" of 1912.

There are three main orders of change here. There are, first, those forced on Hardy by the need to avoid offending the more prudish sections of his audience. Second, there are those made by his own decision, notably for the 1895 and 1912 editions, as he amended names, locations and distances in an effort to make the geography of Wessex more coherent and consistent, both within and between novels. Third, and often most fascinating, there

the landscape, the Square of Pegasus *creeps* round to the north-west, Vega *sparkles* like a lamp. The "roll of the world eastward is almost a palpable movement" (2), while the planet continues its "stately progress" through the stars. In the midst of this grandeur, Gabriel Oak, "unaided and alone", is engaged in his own "progress" as a farmer.

The shifts of temporal and spatial scale here might seem to withdraw all significance from the lonely shepherd, making him of little more account than the "speck of life" he carries into his hut to be revived by its warmth. Yet the passage suggests unity more than disruption. Looking up, the observer sees that the Great Bear (the constellation Ursa Major) has "swung round" the North Star; on the hillside, Gabriel's "steady

---

are those which reflect a refuelling of his creative energies as he worked on the texts, and felt compelled to re-imagine and rewrite characters and situations.

The editor of *Far from the Madding Crowd* has to consider all three kinds of change. Most modern texts follow the 1912 edition, the last to be overseen by Hardy himself, but two of the most widely read have a different editorial policy. Suzanne Falck-Yi's Oxford World's Classics edition (1993) uses the substantives (essentially, the words) of the 1912 edition, but returns to the manuscript for the punctuation (or 'accidentals'), on the grounds that printers and compositors regularly imposed their own house style on Hardy's typically light punctuation. It also prints a number of manuscript passages excluded from the *Cornhill* at

swings and turns in and about his flock" have their own "elements of grace", and in the course of the novel he will prove as quietly enduring as Norcombe Hill itself. Consciousness of the vast movement of the earth is "derived from a tiny frame", but the point works both ways: without the human frame there would be no consciousness.

Moreover, human consciousness is creative rather than passive. It is "the instinctive act of humankind" to discriminate all the sounds the narrator reports, and then reunite them as the "antiphonies of a cathedral choir". It is an essentially human act to do what Oak does, and add to them with the sounds of his own flute-playing. It is the human mind which views the heavens as a beautiful "work of art", or more

---

Stephen's request, and never restored by Hardy, either because he deferred to Stephen's judgement, or because he no longer had access to the manuscript.

These include much of the sheep-shearing-supper (Stephen thought this too long), a description of Troy's adventures after his supposed drowning, and four remarkable paragraphs describing Fanny and her child in their coffin, in which the baby's cheeks and little fists irresistibly remind Bathsheba of "the soft convexity of mushrooms on a dewy morning". Whether Stephen objected to this passage on aesthetic grounds, or because he wished to limit reference to Fanny's "fallen" status, is an open question; perhaps both reasons played their part.

The World's Classics edition is thus an "eclectic" text; it may (or may not) be as

prosaically estimates the time by the position of the stars. The universe is vast and ancient, but it is also one, and we describe it by reference to our physical selves: "the twinkling of the stars seemed to be but throbs of one body, timed by a common pulse".

Hardy's view of "Nature", then, admits a paradox. Human beings and their concerns may appear small and fleeting in comparison with the external world, but they may also take on some of its grandeur; they may even count for more. At the end of the chapter, Gabriel turns from the stars to investigate what proves to be a lantern, which gives him his second glimpse of Bathsheba. She yawns; he yawns in sympathy. It is a tiny gesture to set against the magnitudes of stellar space, but it is

close as we can get to Hardy's intentions, but it remains one that Hardy himself never saw. Rosemarie Morgan and Shannon Russell's Penguin edition (2000) is based wholly on the manuscript, bypassing Stephen's emendations, but also excluding later changes made by Hardy himself. The most striking of the many differences between this and other editions relates to what usually appears as Chapter 16 of the novel, recounting Fanny and Troy's aborted attempt at marriage. This was not in the manuscript, but written on the proofs for the *Cornhill*; accordingly, in the Penguin edition it appears as an appendix, rather than in the body of the text. Similarly, the "slight romance" of Troy's illegitimate but noble birth, introduced in the 1877 one-volume edition and also a sign of the reciprocity that will grow between them, mature into love, and determine their future lives. That too is part of the common pulse of the universe.

## How realistic is Hardy's portrayal of rural life?

In the 1895 preface to *Far from the Madding Crowd* Hardy wrote of Wessex as "a partly real, partly dream-country". In context, he meant only that while the physical descriptions were based on real locations, he had occasionally adjusted a distance or direction, or conflated the features of several different buildings, but critics and

retained in all later texts, appears in the Penguin edition only in the notes.

Editors continue to debate the issues involved, and some of Hardy's revisions are noticed elsewhere in this guide. Perhaps the key point is that Hardy's text was never definitive – he was still marking possible changes in his study copy of *Far from the Madding Crowd* as late as the 1920s, 50 years after it was

written – but constantly in motion. References in this guide are to Robert Schweik's Norton Critical Edition (1986), based on the 1912 Wessex Edition but incorporating some revisions; it includes maps, helpful annotation, discussion of significant textual changes, useful contextual material, and a range of reviews as well as more recent critical essays on the novel ∎

historians have gone further, to question how truthfully the novels represent the "real history" of the region, in an period of agricultural decline, increasing urbanisation, and widespread social change.

Hardy's early readers preferred to dwell on what they took to be the timeless aspects of English rural life. They had some grounds for doing so. *Far from the Madding Crowd* appeared in 1874, when the National Agricultural Labourers' Union led by Joseph Arch was, as Arch put it, "flowing over the country like a spring tide", with more than a thousand branches, a national membership of 72,000, and a weekly journal selling 30,000 copies an issue. The landowners and the Church came out against the Union; the Bishop of Gloucester thought unionists should be ducked in the village horse ponds.

But none of this finds an echo in *Far from the Madding Crowd*, even though Hardy had heard Arch speak in Dorchester in 1873. One of the platforms of the Union was its opposition to the annual hiring fairs, but the one Gabriel attends prompts no overt political comment. Arch warned of the precarious position of tenant farmers like Bathsheba – some 400 in the Dorset area had gone bankrupt in just a few years – but Bathsheba gives her new employees a 10 shilling bonus, roughly a week's wages. As an inexperienced woman farmer she needs their goodwill, but this is still an extraordinary gesture in a region notorious for paying well below the national average. Her workforce apparently knows nothing of strikes, arson, or Joseph Arch. Understandably, *The Times* described the novel as an "idyl, or pastoral poem".

The set-piece descriptions of shearing in the Great Barn and the supper which follows seem to support this view. Unlike the medieval church or castle, the barn still serves the purpose for which it was designed: it "embodied practices which had suffered no mutilation at the hands of time" (22). In comparison with cities, Weatherbury appears "immutable"; at the shearing-supper the workers lean against one another "as at suppers in the early ages of the world". Nature and culture are so far at one – "the barn was natural to the shearers, and the shearers were in harmony with the barn" – that work seems to be done almost without effort.

These are passages of great charm, and there is no missing Hardy's affection for the world they evoke. Yet even here, class and economic tensions make themselves felt. Pennyways, the former bailiff dismissed for thieving, is an uninvited guest at the supper. The table is so placed that it extends into the house, allowing Bathsheba to sit at its head "without mingling with the men"; Gabriel, asked to preside at the other end, outdoors, has to give up his place on the arrival of Boldwood, his social superior.

This incident is emblematic. It is one part of

Gabriel's role in the novel to remind the reader of the economic realities of Wessex life: the twopence he pays so Bathsheba can pass through the tollgate – too small a sum to haggle over, unlike threepence, which is "an appreciable infringement on a day's wages"; the loss of his uninsured sheep and subsequent fall from farmer back to shepherd; his playing the flute for pennies at the hiring fair ("a small fortune to a destitute man"); the cost of a shepherd's crook (two shillings); the "trifle" he gives to Fanny (one shilling – the price of an issue of the *Cornhill,* like the one in the reader's hand); the value of Bathsheba's stacks of wheat and barley (£750); his "coming it quite the dand", with a horse to ride and "shining boots with hardly a hob in 'em", when he enters into partnership with the lovesick Boldwood.

Troy's recklessness contrasts with Oak's thrift. He leaves Bathsheba fearful that she will be unable to meet her rent when it falls due, loses more than £100 gambling on horses, and spends all he has, £27, on Fanny's tombstone. Even death has its precise cost: when Fanny dies destitute in the Union workhouse, the parish is obliged to pay half a crown for her grave, but not the shilling required to toll the bells; "the bell's a luxury: but 'a can hardly do without the grave, poor thing" (42). *Far from the Madding Crowd* may be a pastoral novel, but it is one in which every coin is counted.

The key point has been well made by Penny

Boumelha:

> Rural society, for Hardy, is just that: a *society*, in
> which exploitation, solidarity, and the struggle
> for survival are experienced quite as keenly as
> they are in urban settings.

The Weatherbury community is a relatively settled
one, but it is neither idyllic nor timeless: Fanny
dies in poverty, Joseph is a drunkard, and Cainy
Ball is a child worker, even if Gabriel makes a
kindly master. The two figures who do most to
threaten rural stability, Sergeant Troy and Farmer
Boldwood, are both native to the area; the two who
help put it to rights, Gabriel and Bathsheba, are
both recent arrivals – the former a self-made man
twice over, who makes a prudent as well as a loving
marriage, the latter the daughter of a gentleman-
tailor (and "very celebrated bankrupt"), whose
incautious first marriage almost costs her the farm.
The social criticism in *Far from the Madding
Crowd* is more muted than it was to be in later
novels, the representation of work and community
more celebratory, but even in his most compliant
mood, anxious to please Leslie Stephen and to win
a new audience, Hardy could not wholly turn his
back on the darker sides of rural life.

# Is Gabriel Oak a hero?

For many readers Gabriel Oak's status as the hero of *Far from the Madding Crowd* is beyond question. Formally, he is the character with whom the novel begins, and he marries its heroine at the end; morally and psychologically, he appears to set the standard by which other characters are judged. So, for example, the narrator contrasts his "manly resolve" with Boldwood's instability, while Bathsheba envies the fortitude with which he puts aside matters affecting only his "personal well-being": "That was how she would wish to be" (43).

Robert Langbaum, perhaps Oak's greatest admirer, argues that his heroism is in fact threefold. As a shepherd who plays the flute, he is the very definition of a pastoral hero; in Warren's Malthouse, with four lambs hanging over his shoulders, he looks the "epitome of the world's health and vigour" (15). Within the limits of the pastoral form, he is a hero of romance, playing the part of faithful squire to Bathsheba's cruel lady (this is the "dumb, devoted passion" which so exasperated Henry James); and he emerges as a hero in what Langbaum calls "the new realistic mode", who meets setbacks in work and love with patience and self-control.

*Opposite: Julie Christie (Bathsheba) and Alan Bates (Oak) in Schlesinger's 1967 film*

For others, however, Oak's rightness is less clear-cut. His initial assessment of Bathsheba's "vanity" is summary and inadequate; he is given to spying on her in the early chapters, and to criticising her conduct in the later ones; and his proposal of marriage leaves her amused and obliged to stifle a yawn, in sharp contrast to her arousal before Troy. To Rosemarie Morgan – Oak's fiercest critic – he is less a moral example than a moral censor, whose "induction of guilt and fear" in a previously spirited and vibrant woman crushes her into conformity.

Neither of these positions allows enough for the fact that Oak changes in the course of the novel. He is an example of that notorious problem for the novelist, of how to make the nice people good and the good people interesting, and the opening pages show Hardy feeling his way to a solution. The first four paragraphs of the novel, with the comparison of Oak's smile to "the rays in a rudimentary sketch of the sun", and the comic business of his watch, seem designed to patronise him, but that view is immediately set against what more "thoughtful persons" might observe: a man of potentially "imposing" presence who chooses to walk "unassumingly", trusting to his "capacity to wear well" rather than to appearances. Like Norcombe Hill, on which he is seen at work in the second chapter, he is an "ordinary specimen", who yet has a power of endurance which grander or more ambitious figures may lack.

At the same time, however, the contention that his face still shows "the curves and hues of youth", while his modesty "would have become a vestal", suggests that Oak, now 28 years old, has come late to sexual maturity. The solitude, hard work and self-denial needed to rise from shepherd to farmer, we may infer, have hitherto kept desire at bay. Now, on the point of success, and beginning to feel "the want of a satisfactory form to fill an increasing void within him", he settles on Bathsheba as the one satisfying "form". In his autobiography, Hardy wrote of his own "late development in virility", describing himself as "a child till he was sixteen, a youth till he was five-and-twenty, and a young man till he was fifty". Oak, in these terms, has barely reached manhood. He gazes at Bathsheba not, as Morgan argues, as a voyeur, but with the helpless infatuation of a youth.

His sexual diffidence does him no favours with Bathsheba. He blushes, concedes her superior cleverness ("I can't match you, I know" (3)), and becomes tongue-tied. Her movements have the "rapidity" of the kingfisher and the "noiselessness" of the hawk, his are as "slow" and "steady" as "the eastward roll of the earth", and the impulsive Bathsheba is not to be won by slow steadiness. When he holds her hand he is afraid of being "too demonstrative", and touches her fingers "with the lightness of a small-hearted person". He himself notices that he waits for her presence in much the same way as his dog waits for his meals. When she says she needs someone to "tame" her, and does not love him, he can only reply that he loves her, "and, as for myself, I am content to be liked".

The comedy of this is complicated in two ways. There is first what the narrator calls the "genuine pathos" of Oak's declaration:

> *I shall do one thing in this life – one thing certain – that is, love you, and long for you, and* keep wanting you *till I die. (4)*

Many of Hardy's lovers say something like this; in Oak's case, it proves to be true. Second, his uncertainty with Bathsheba contrasts with his skill and authority as a working man. This is not fully apparent at the outset, since he twice falls asleep when he needed to be wakeful: once in his hut, when he neglects to open the ventilator and only Bathsheba's prompt action saves him from suffocation, and then after her departure, when he neglects to call in his dogs, yields to "the luxury of bed", and wakes to discover that the younger dog has driven his entire flock over a precipice to their deaths in the chalk pit below.

This is the turning point in Oak's life. In Hardy's fiction a character's mental state is often revealed not by analysis but by what they see: in this instance, a tortured landscape, in which "the attenuated skeleton of a chrome-yellow moon" hangs over an "oval pool" which glitters "like a dead man's eye", and a breeze twists the reflection of the morning star into "a phosphoric streak upon the water" (5). "All this Oak saw and remembered." The image is one of desolation: ten years of work, and all his savings, have been wiped out in a few careless moments. But Oak "wears well". By the following chapter, two months later, he has cleared his debts and is looking for work, a sadder and more meditative man, who has "passed through an ordeal of wretchedness" but acquired "a dignified calm he had never before known".

With the logic of romance, in which events often fall into groups of three, he now falls asleep a third time, in the back of a wagon, and wakes to find himself again in Bathsheba's world. In directing the effort to put out the fire, he shows qualities of energy and leadership which will remain with him throughout the novel. The youth has become a man, not only able but willing to impose himself, and resourceful enough, over the next two years, to remake himself as "Farmer Oak", and to win Bathsheba.

The second of these tasks is the more painful, since he has to watch as she turns first to Boldwood and then to Troy. Gabriel's situation intrigued Hardy sufficiently for him to return to it in two later novels, with Diggory Venn in *The Return of the Native*, and Elizabeth-Jane in *The*

*Mayor of Casterbridge.* All three are at first rejected by their future partners, and have to accept a position as the second spouse, taken on only after the first has proved feckless or unfaithful. All three suffer social and economic setbacks; all are naturally thrifty, having learned, like Elizabeth-Jane, to live "in the rear of opportunity"; they are habitual and often critical observers, mindful of the common good, and correspondingly wary of the demand for individual fulfilment. Their collective outlook is neatly encapsulated in the first of the malthouse scenes, when Gabriel is offered some bread and bacon, with the caution that it has been dropped in the road and might be gritty:

> *"Don't ye chaw quite close, shepherd... Don't let your teeth quite meet, and you won't feel the sandiness at all. Ah! 'tis wonderful what can be done by contrivance!" (8)*

Oak, like Diggory and Elizabeth-Jane, is willing not to "chaw quite close". Hardy's poem 'He Never Expected Much' (see opposite), written on his 86th birthday and, despite the title, in the first person, suggests that he understood and sympathised with such temperaments.

Gabriel's ability to make much out of little allows him to feel "the luxury of content" (22) merely by being close to Bathsheba. In the sheep-shearing scene, "that his bright lady and himself formed one group, exclusively their own, and containing no others in the world, was enough" – the description of Bathsheba as his "bright lady" again evoking the literary form of the romance. His contentment, however, is short-lived. Boldwood intrudes on his group of two with Bathsheba, and a moment later he nips the ewe he is shearing in the groin.

This both is and is not an accident. Long before Freud spelled out the idea in *The Psychopathology of Everyday Life* (1901), Hardy recognised that, in Freud's words, actions which appear accidental "have a meaning and can be interpreted, and one is justified in inferring from them the presence of restrained or repressed impulses and intentions". Oak's slip can fairly be read as retaliation for the wound Bathsheba has inflicted on him, all the more so since Hardy himself equates the two:

'NE NEVER EXPECTED MUCH'

———————

Well, world, you have kept
          faith with me,
Kept faith with me;
Upon the whole you have
          proved to be
Much as you said you were...

'I do not promise overmuch,
Child, overmuch;
Just neutral-tinted haps and
          such',
You said to minds like mine.
Wise warning for your
          credit's sake!
Which I for one failed not to
          take,
And hence could stem such
          strain and ache
As each year might assign ∎

*she herself was the cause of the poor ewe's wound,*
*because she had wounded the ewe's shearer in a still*
*more vital part. (22)*

If this gives some credence to Rosemarie Morgan's view that Gabriel belongs to the dark "world of male violence" signalled by Troy's sword, crop and whip, or Boldwood's heavy stick and double-barrelled gun, the scene also hints for the first time at an erotic charge between Oak and Bathsheba. It is she who remarks, provocatively, that the ewe he has just turned on to its back, its pink skin newly exposed, "blushes at the insult" (her identification with the shorn ewes is underlined when they are

## THE ORIGINS OF THE WESSEX NOVEL

"Greenhill was the Nijnii Novgorod of [South] Wessex; and the busiest, merriest, noisiest day of the whole statute number was the day of the sheep fair." In this sentence, in Chapter 50 of *Far from the Madding Crowd*, Hardy reintroduced to English literature the almost forgotten name of Wessex.

It has, then, some importance in literary history, and indeed in social history; nearly 900 local companies and services in the current Dorset business directory incorporate "Wessex" in their name, in tribute to Hardy rather than in memory of the kingdom in south-west England to which

marked with her initials, "B.E."), while the narrator's reference to her "dominative and tantalizing graciousness" – far from the simplicity Victorian readers expected in their heroines – underlines the note of sexual challenge. The episode is at once realistic and symbolic, in keeping with a note Hardy made in 1886:

> My art is to intensify the expression of things... so that the heart and inner meaning becomes visible.

It is an art he was to develop in later novels, as in the threshing-machine and Stonehenge chapters

---

the name belonged in Anglo-Saxon times. There is even an Earl of Wessex, the title assumed in 1999 by Prince Edward; the original title lapsed in 1071, and might have been lost to history had Hardy not revived it in fiction.

In a miniature way the sentence is characteristic of Hardy's position as a regional writer. In the description that follows of the bustle and merriment of the sheep fair, the narrator associates himself not only with the countrymen who were its regular visitors, but also with those urban readers for whom Hardy's Greenhill and Nijnii Novgorod resemble each other not least in that they were places to read about but scarcely to visit.

He is both an eager authority on matters of local knowledge and custom, confidently distinguishing various breeds of sheep by noting the "vermiculated horns" of the one and the "dark and heavy horns" of another, and the well-informed reader of the *Cornhill*, who can refer in

in *Tess of the d'Urbervilles* (and an art Lawrence was to learn from him, as in the 'Rabbit' chapter of *Women in Love*). Here he reveals layers of unstated and barely recognised feeling between his two central characters – desire and anger on Gabriel's side, advance and retreat on Bathsheba's – which it will take the rest of the novel to resolve.

In the following chapters Oak's part is secondary, as attention shifts to Bathsheba's entanglement with Troy and subsequent rejection of Boldwood, but he is never long out of sight. The negative side of his capacity to live with lowered expectations is felt in his attempt to impose a

passing to the site of the annual Makaryev Fair, and trade centre of the Russian empire. In his justly influential essay (see p.76), Raymond Williams describes Hardy as simultaneously a "passionate participant" in the values and traditions of his region, and an "educated observer" of them.

What it meant for Hardy to occupy this border country needs further comment, but Chapter 50 introduces two other aspects of Hardy's Wessex fiction. Wessex is, first, a place where violent juxtapositions and coincidences can and do occur. Troy, believed drowned, is about to return to the story, under the eyes of his wife Bathsheba, disguised as a circus rider dressed as the highwayman Dick Turpin.

Thus concealed he is even able to steal a note that has been given to her, and one of the two running titles to the chapter – 'Troy Touches His Wife's Hand' – underlines the coincidence. The "Wessex" names – Casterbridge for Dorchester, Greenhill for Woodbury Hill, Budmouth for Weymouth, and so on – signal the reader's entry into

similar morality on Bathsheba, when he tells her, in effect, that her moment of folly in sending the valentine to Boldwood has placed her under a lifetime obligation to him. It is Boldwood's interrogation which prompts Bathsheba's protest: "It is difficult for a woman to define her feelings in language which is chiefly made by men to express theirs"(51).

But it might equally have been made in reply to Gabriel's complaint that her conduct has been "unworthy of any thoughtful, and meek, and comely woman": why should Bathsheba, or indeed any woman, because she is "comely", also be

---

not only to a physical region but also to an imaginative space where a range of fictional conventions operate at Hardy's will, including the unspoken rule that the events will unfold within a determined boundary. Those who leave invariably return – Troy in this novel, Clym, Susan Henchard, Grace Melbury, Arabella, in later ones – and their return is always disruptive.

Second, Wessex is also a place where events in the foreground may ultimately count for relatively little. The other running title to Chapter 50 is 'The Sheep Fair', and what Joseph Poorgrass remembers the occasion for is not Troy's return, but that he helped to carry the "body" of Black Bess, Turpin's famous horse, out of the arena: "'Twill be something to talk of at Warren's in future years, Jan, and hand down to our children." And for years to come he tells, "with the air of a man who had had experiences in his time", how he once touched the hoof of Black Bess.

The Wessex of the novels is not only a territory but also and more importantly a

"meek"? Whatever his intentions, Oak's argument is oppressive here; he is ready to sacrifice his own hope of happiness, but he also risks hers. That he is alive to the faults in Troy's nature but blind to those in Boldwood further underlines that he is not, for all his merits, the unequivocal moral centre of the novel.

Oak's willingness to face facts, however, rather than merely wish them other than they are, is evident in one of the great setpieces in the novel, the summer storm which threatens Bathsheba's ricks, and destroys Boldwood's. The evolutionary scientist Thomas Huxley, whom Hardy admired as

community, which exists as a community because it shares a collection of stories. To know Wessex, or to belong to it, is to know these stories, and to understand the need for their repeated telling. As they are told and retold, the uniquely personal experience yields in importance to the shared experience of the community.

But at this stage of Hardy's career Wessex existed only in rudimentary form. The preface he wrote for *Far from the Madding Crowd* in 1895, for the Osgood, McIlvaine edition of what were now to be known as the 'Wessex Novels', reads back into the past a conception which in fact emerged in more piecemeal fashion. Hardy recalled: "The series of novels I projected being mainly of the kind called local, they seemed to require a territorial definition of some sort to lend unity to their scene." But in 1874 he had no thought of planning a "series"; it was only gradually, as he became preoccupied with what Simon Gatrell nicely calls "the recording of unrecorded history", that he felt the need to revisit and

a man of "fearless mind", compared the natural world to a game of chess:

> The chess-board is the world, the pieces are the phenomena of the universe, the rules of the game are what we call the laws of Nature. The player on the other side is hidden from us. We know that his play is always fair, just and patient. But we also know, to our cost, that he never overlooks a mistake, or makes the smallest allowance for ignorance... one who plays ill is checkmated – without haste, but without remorse.

criss-cross the same territory.

There was a precedent for doing so in Trollope's 'Chronicles of Barsetshire', written between 1855 and 1867, but Trollope had a very different relation to his material.

In his *Autobiography* he records that while he was writing *Framley Parsonage* (the fourth of the six novels) he "made a map of the dear county", and that "each fictitious site" represented "a spot of which I know all the accessories, as though I had lived and wandered there".

That "as though" marks the difference from Hardy, who precisely *had* lived there. And, by the end of the century, an increasing number of people were anxious to wander there, as Hardy acknowledged not only in the various prefaces but also by providing a map of Wessex for the 1895 edition, together with illustrations "drawn on the spot". 'Wessex' had become in effect a brand name: not just the world Hardy happened to write about, and one that he valued, but what he brought to the literary marketplace ∎

Those who understand the rules, and don't expect them to be suspended for their own benefit, can at least keep the game going, as Gabriel does when Nature provides him with a series of clues about the coming storm, in the behaviour of toads, garden slugs, spiders and sheep. At one point, while trying to protect the stack, he wonders whether to retreat to safety, or to work on regardless of the risk: "Was his life so valuable to him after all?" (37). Characteristically, he resolves to "stick to the stack", but takes the precaution of improvising a lightning conductor; a few moments later it saves both his and Bathsheba's life. In a dynamic that Conrad was to place at the centre of his fiction, Gabriel survives both an external "infuriated universe" and his own inner doubts by attending to facts, and to work.

# How should we read the ending of *Far from the Madding Crowd*?

Gabriel's heroism in the storm scene is unequivocal. The literal flashes of lightning about him recall the figurative language of "a firmament of light, and of sharp hisses, resembling a sky-full of meteors" (28) used to describe Troy's sword display in the hollow amid the ferns, and the contrast works to Gabriel's advantage: unlike Troy he faces real danger to his life, his actions are disinterested, not for show, and he works alongside Bathsheba rather than requiring her to remain still and submissive. The key chapter, titled 'The Storm – The Two Together', offers further hints of a latent erotic connection between them as they battle to save the ricks: at one moment Oak feels Bathsheba's "warm arm tremble in his hand"(37), at another "a zephyr curling about his cheek", which proves to be her breath as she follows him to the barn, and "she speaks more warmly to him" than at any previous time. These are intimations of what the narrator will later describe as "romance growing up in the interstices of a mass of hard prosaic reality", and it is essential to the conclusion of the novel that this phrase should be grounded in detail, as it is here, not merely offered for the reader to take on trust.

The next sequence of the novel – in the serial version, the September, October and November instalments – covers Fanny's death, Troy's disappearance, and the renewal of Boldwood's courtship of Bathsheba. Again Oak takes second place in the narrative, without ever quite being forgotten. Bathsheba visits his cottage to ask what he knows about Fanny, but seeing him kneel to pray does not approach him; it is he who brings back Fanny's coffin, and rubs out the words "and child". Later, Bathsheba confides to him her uncertainty about whether to agree to Boldwood's plea for a secret engagement. Their conversation is formal – he calls her "ma'am", she slips back and forth between "Gabriel" and "Mr. Oak" – but she is secretly "ruffled" that he makes no mention of his own continuing love for her: "That was the insect sting" (51). There is a profound ambiguity in her feelings here, of a kind Hardy was to explore further in later novels, notably *The Woodlanders* and *Tess*.

Consciously, she disavows love as "an utterly bygone, sorry, worn-out miserable thing"; her experience with Troy has left her so weary that she is ready to marry Boldwood as an act of "penance". At the same time, in "the centermost parts of her complicated heart", she is already preparing to "rally", in unconscious obedience to what Hardy calls, in *Tess*, the "irresistible, universal, automatic tendency to find sweet pleasure somewhere, which pervades all life". Some reminder of Oak's love would have been "pretty and sweet"; she is sure she would have rejected it, but the reader is entitled to wonder.

These hints of potential erotic feeling between the two bear on how we read the end of the novel. In the penultimate paragraph, we are told that "Oak laughed, and Bathsheba smiled (for she never laughed readily now)" (57). A number of critics have taken this to suggest that her marriage to Oak is a kind of defeat, entered into only because she has lost the will to manage her farm without him: that, as Lawrence puts it in words not unlike her own, "the flower of imaginative love is dead for her with Troy's scorn of her". This reading has some force, but it runs against the grain of the pastoral form, with its implicit faith in the capacity for renewal in the human as well as in the natural world, and it ignores the subtlety with which Hardy records her fluctuating feelings. Chapter 56 begins: "Bathsheba revived with the spring" – and the following few pages are devoted to exploring what revival means.

At the outset her "old colour" has given way to "preternatural" paleness, she keeps indoors, and prefers to be alone; then, overhearing children learning a new hymn (as it happens, one of Hardy's own favourites) she is "stirred by emotions" she had thought dead in her. Her reaction is a flood of tears, which comes as a "luxury" rather than a "scourge"; the intensity of feeling, however inchoate, is itself a relief, as it is in the great 19th-century poems of depression and *ennui*, from Wordsworth and Coleridge to Tennyson and Arnold.

The news that Oak intends to leave distresses Bathsheba, but it also breaks into the "chronic gloom of her life", turning her mind outwards to the question of his possible reasons for doing so. The explanation, evident to the reader before it is to Bathsheba – that he is anxious to protect her from local gossip that he is "sniffing about" waiting for a chance to marry her – is an echo of the mingled delicacy and awkwardness that he displayed in the opening chapters of the novel. Their constraint when she calls on him recalls "the days when they were strangers", and this too is significant. When they sit in his cottage, the firelight dances on the old furniture, "all a-sheenen / Wi' long years o' handlen", in the words Hardy quotes from William Barnes's finest poem, "Woak Hill".

The emphasis is on the healing power of continuity, of things loved all the more because they have always been loved. Bathsheba and Oak are finding their way back to where they once had been, and are preparing to begin anew: hence Gabriel's wish that on the morning of their wedding she should arrange her hair "as she had worn it years ago on Norcombe Hill", and her "rejuvenated" appearance, her cheeks again "incarnadined" – a recollection of the elaborate description of her blushes in Chapter Three. It is "As though a rose should shut and be a bud again".

The quotation, from Keats's "The Eve of St Agnes", is aptly chosen. A rose cannot bloom and then become a bud again; life does not admit of perfect returns, and recovery is not the same as innocence. Bathsheba has been hurt, and the scars will remain. Keats's line both summons the romance of the imagination, and concedes, in the two words "As though", the power of ordinary reality. Hardy's novel ends with a similar balance, and a small verbal joke: a marriage in which, to Gabriel at least, Bathsheba is still "remarkably like the girl of that fascinating dream" on Norcombe Hill, is accomplished a sentence or two later "in a remarkably short space of time". It is both a wonderful and an everyday event, celebrated by Keats's poem of enchantment, and by the "hideous clang of music" from the worm-eaten instruments of the "true and original Weatherbury band". Joseph Poorgrass has the last word, and for once it is pertinent:

> *"since 'tis as 'tis, why, it might have been worse, and I feel my thanks accordingly".*

# HARDY AND THE CRITICAL TRADITION

The first readers of *Far from the Madding Crowd* encountered the novel as a magazine story by an unknown author, with no expectations other than that it would match the high standards usual in the *Cornhill*. By contrast, the modern reader usually comes to it as an edited "text", complete with introductory essay and explanatory notes, in a series with the word "Classic" in its name, and the heavy cultural freight that word carries. Hardy, the format suggests, belongs among the "great" or "classic" writers.

But Hardy's classic status was hard-won. Critics have been unsure what to make of him, while two other 'great' novelists, Virginia Woolf and D. H. Lawrence, found themselves conflicted in their response to his work. In their accounts, Hardy succeeds almost in spite of himself. Troy, according to Lawrence, is the only man in the novel who "knows anything" about Bathsheba; Hardy's failure to recognise this is a mark of his "bad art", leaving it to the reader, in this case Lawrence, to uncover the truth Hardy has unconsciously revealed, but because of his preconceived view of life has also missed or disguised. Woolf, too, finds Hardy's achievement somehow accidental: the reader's part is to "put aside the writer's conscious intention in favour of some deeper intention of which perhaps he may be unconscious". It is these unconscious intuitions which give readers "the most profound sense of satisfaction".

It is astonishing to find two novelists suggesting of a third that art, or craft, had nothing to do with his success, but the assumption that Hardy was an involuntary or unconscious writer has proved hard to shake off. One of the most influential critics of the 20th century, F. R. Leavis, wrote scathingly of Hardy in *The Great Tradition* (1948) as lacking the "rightness with which the great novelists show their profound sureness of their essential purpose". For Leavis, the literature of the great tradition is marked by "a vital capacity for experience, a kind of reverent openness before life, and a marked moral intensity". These in turn, claims Leavis, emerge from a unified creative intelligence, and this unity of being is lacking in Hardy: rather than being integrated with it, his moral seriousness is imposed upon what his creative imagination discovers, and as a result his novels are "gauche" and "clumsy".

The note of condescension in these approaches is as unmissable as it is unwarranted, but even Hardy's more recent admirers cannot let go the idea that he is at his best when least in control of what he is doing. John Bayley, in his introduction to the New Wessex edition of *Far from the*

*Madding Crowd*, describes Hardy as working "without apparent volition", "involuntarily", "naturally", with an "unselfconscious capacity" to feel with the human beings he represents, and so on. Bayley is, however, more willing than earlier critics to identify the moments of success, and to offer an explanation of them. The key term in his introduction is "incongruity": the incongruity of life, with its surprises and chance collocations of events, and a matching incongruity of style. This, for example, from the scene in the hollow amid the ferns, when Troy spits a caterpillar that has crawled on to Bathsheba's dress:

> *She saw the point glisten towards her bosom and seemingly enter it. Bathsheba closed her eyes in full persuasion that she was killed at last. However, feeling just as usual, she opened them again. (28)*

The two sentences manage to be at once climactic, with the striking use of "glisten" as a verb of motion, and almost comically flat ("However, feeling just as usual..."). It seems not unreasonable to say that the rightness of this, as well as its oddity, is both "Hardyesque" and instinctive; the effect, that is to say, doesn't seem to have been looked for, but simply found. What makes it impressive is that it is so deeply linked to the sense the novel gives of a world experienced with near-tragic intensity, by characters who are also seen as ordinary, living in a universe which has no regard for them.

Bayley argues that if George Eliot and Dickens had written a comparable scene, they would have tried to be "too much in charge". Hardy, on the other hand, is content to write - here, at least; Bayley takes a different view of the later novels - as if he were merely "the mouthpiece of dramatic events and violent emotions". Perhaps this suggests a more helpful way to approach Hardy's supposed "unconsciousness". It derives not from an absence of art but from his faith in the power of "story", best exemplified in another "great tradition", that of the English and Scottish popular ballads, in which the nearness of love and hate, hope and fear, life and death, is assumed without comment. Hardy's formal and stylistic incongruities stand in close, deliberate and necessary relation with his sense of life as an inextricable mix of the comic and the tragic.

# TWO CONTRASTING VIEWS ON
# *FAR FROM THE MADDING CROWD*

---

"Mr Hardy's novel is... inordinately diffuse, and, as a piece of narrative, singularly inartistic... The chief purpose of the book is, we suppose, to represent Gabriel's dumb, devoted passion, his biding his time, his rendering unsuspected services to the woman who has scorned him, his integrity and simplicity and sturdy patience. In all this the tale is very fairly successful... but we cannot say that we either understand or like Bathsheba. She is a young lady of the inconsequential, wilful, mettlesome type which has lately become so much the fashion for heroines... the type which aims at giving one a very intimate sense of a young lady's *womanishness*. But Mr Hardy's embodiment of it seems to us to lack reality... Everything human in the book strikes us as factitious and insubstantial; the only things we believe in are the sheep and the dogs. But, as we say, Mr Hardy has gone astray very cleverly, and his superficial novel is a really curious imitation of something better."

**Henry James**, at the time working on *Roderick Hudson*, his first novel after leaving America, reviewed *Far from the Madding Crowd* for The *Nation* (24 December 1874)

"So it is that upon Bathsheba's vulnerability, her pain, her passion, Hardy's sympathies turn and turn again. The centre of caring feeling and intense emotion is quintessentially the flow between author and heroine, even at the last, where Bathsheba is but a ghost of her former self. No longer freely riding out, no longer exploring the world about her – the cities, the market-places, the world of work and men – no longer resourcefully participating in the life of her estate, but instead, joylessly auditing book ledgers in the reduced space that is now her confined domain, Bathsheba's fearless spirit is finally broken...

Bathsheba's perpetual exposure to the world of male violence, her unknowing proximity to something dark and brutal in Oak's world, draws us into a deep, shadowy region of *Far from the Madding Crowd* where the Hardy, who so dearly loved the voluptuous Tess of his later novel, lovingly dwells. His vibrant, self-delighting, energetic heroine whose resourcefulness and strength sustain a family property, a labour force and a farming community, blossoms into womanhood, ventures into business, into marriage, into the world of men, and is nullified. And Hardy is the lone mourner."

**Rosemarie Morgan**, in *Women and Sexuality in the Novels of Thomas Hardy* (1988)

# A SHORT CHRONOLOGY

1840 Born in Higher Bockhampton near Dorchester, first of four children of Thomas Hardy, a builder and stonemason, and his wife Jemima.

1850 His serious schooldays begin when he is enrolled into a school set up in Dorchester by Isaac Last, a clever Noncomformist headmaster. Learns Latin and – a "born bookworm", as he called himself – reads voraciously.

1856 Becomes an apprentice to the Dorchester architect, John Hicks. Continues his studies at home and begins to learn Greek.

1856 Aged 16, joins the crowds to see Martha Browne hanged for murder at Dorchester Gaol. He never forgot the experience. "I am ashamed to say I saw her hanged," he wrote in a letter when he was an old man; his only excuse was he was young, he added. "I remember what a fine figure she showed against the sky as she hung in the misty rain, and how the tight black silk gown set off her shape as she wheeled half-round and back."

1862 Moves to London to work for a distinguished architect, Arthur Blomfield.

1867 Begins work on his first (unpublished) novel, *The Poor Man and the Lady*.

1870 Meets Emma Gifford, his future wife, while restoring St Juliot's church in north Cornwall.

1872 *Under the Greenwood Tree* published, receives good reviews.

1873 Horace Moule, the son of a minister and Hardy's closest and most influential childhood friend, commits suicide by cutting his throat. He was a depressive. "Never again would Hardy have a friend who held his heart so wholly," writes Claire Tomalin.

1871 *Desperate Remedies* published.

1874 *Far from the Madding Crowd* serialised and published as a book, a year after the publication of *A Pair of Blue Eyes*. Marries Emma at St Peter's, Paddington. The honeymoon is spent in France.

1878 *The Return of the Native.* Though not really a clubbable man, he joins the Savile Club. Later also becomes a member of the Athenæum. As his fame spreads, he becomes an established figure in the literary world, meeting Henry James, Matthew Arnold, Tennyson and Browning.

1885 The Hardys move into Max Gate, the house they have built in Dorset. *The Mayor of Casterbridge* completed.

1887 *The Woodlanders.*

1890 Visits Paris in August with his brother Henry to show him the sights. These included a visit to the Moulin Rouge to see the can-can performed. Recalling that the Moulin Rouge was close to the cemetery of Montmartre, Hardy writes of himself (in the third person) that "looking down at the young women dancing the cancan, and grimacing at the men ... he could see through some back windows over their heads to the last resting-place of so many similar gay Parisians silent under the moonlight".

1891 *Tess of the d'Urbervilles* published. The passing of the US Copyright Act, as well as the success of *Tess*, makes Hardy rich. He buys two houses in Dorchester, one for his sisters, both now teaching there, and one as an investment.

1895 *Jude the Obscure.* Heavily criticised for its radical views on marriage and Christianity. Some booksellers were said to have wrapped it in brown paper before selling it. "After verdicts from the press its next misfortune was to be burnt by a bishop [the Bishop of Wakefield], probably in his despair at not being able to burn me," Hardy later wrote. *Jude* was his last novel.

1907 Finishes *The Dynasts.*

1910 Awarded the Order of Merit by King George V.

1912 Emma Hardy dies at about 8am on November 27th. It is "the moment when Thomas Hardy became a great poet", says Claire Tomalin. Filled with sorrow and remorse for his coldness in the estrangement which had developed between them, he had her coffin placed at the foot of his bed, where it remained for three days and nights until the funeral.

1914 Marries Florence Dugdale at St Andrew's, Enfield, Middlesex.

1919 Macmillan publish his *Collected Poems*, but his output remains prodigious and he publishes three further volumes of poetry.

1923 Augustus John's portrait of Hardy, showing a face "refined into an essence", as T.E. Lawrence put it. "I don't know whether that is how I look or not – but that is how I *feel*," said Hardy.

1923 July. The Prince of Wales, on a tour of Somerset, Dorset and Wiltshire, has lunch with Hardy and Florence at Max Gate. A retinue of 13 have to be fed in the house, not counting the chauffeurs, while the grandees accompanying the Prince eat under trees in the garden. The Prince "did not pretend to have read anything by his host", says Claire Tomalin, and rural matters were probably discussed. The lunch went well. "I didn't fuss around him," Florence wrote afterwards, "and I think he was grateful. He made himself very much at home... He grew rather gay and jocular... I had been told he ate nothing." In fact he asked for a second helping of ham  and finished up with "a glass of 40-year-old sherry" and a cigar.

1928 January 11, Hardy dies following a heart attack in the evening. Subsequently his ashes are interred in Westminster Abbey and his heart buried at Stinsford.

# FURTHER READING

## Biographies

Hardy, Florence Emily, *The Early Life of Thomas Hardy*,
London: Macmillan, 1928

Hardy, Florence Emily, *The Later Years of Thomas Hardy*,
London: Macmillan, 1930

Gibson, James, *Thomas Hardy: A Literary Life*,
London: Macmillan, 1996

Millgate, Michael, *Thomas Hardy: A Biography Revisited*, Oxford
University Press, 2004

Millgate, Michael, ed, *The Life and Work of Thomas Hardy, by
Thomas Hardy,* London: Macmillan, 1984

Tomalin, Claire, *Thomas Hardy: The Time-Torn Man,*
London: Penguin Viking, 2006

## Companions

Kramer, Dale, ed, *The Cambridge Companion to Thomas Hardy*, Cambridge University Press, 1999

Mallett, Phillip, ed, *Advances in Thomas Hardy Studies*, London: Palgrave Macmillan, 2004

Mallett, Phillip, ed, *Thomas Hardy in Context*, Cambridge University Press, 2013

Morgan, Rosemarie, ed, *Ashgate Research Companion to Thomas Hardy,* Aldershot: Ashgate, 2010

Wilson, Keith, ed, *A Companion to Thomas Hardy*, Oxford: Wiley-Blackwell, 2009

## Critical Studies and Collections

Berger, Sheila, *Thomas Hardy and Visual Structures: Framing, Disruption*, Process, New York University Press, 1990

Brooks, Jean R., *Thomas Hardy: The Poetic Structure,* London: Elek Books, 1971

Bullen, J. B., *The Expressive Eye: Fiction and Perception in the Works of Thomas Hardy*, Oxford: Clarendon Press, 1986

Cosslett, Tess, *The 'Scientific Movement' and Victorian Literature*, Brighton: Harvester Press, 1982

Cox, R.G., ed., *Thomas Hardy: The Critical Heritage*, London: Routledge & Kegan Paul, 1970

Devereux, Joanna, *Patriarchy and its Discontents: Sexual Politics in Selected Novels and Stories of Thomas Hardy*, London: Routledge, 2003

Draper, R.P., ed., *Thomas Hardy: Three Pastoral Novels: a Casebook*, London: Macmillan Education, 1987

Federico, Annette, *Masculine Identity in Hardy and Gissing*, Rutherford: Fairleigh Dickinson University Press, 1991

Guérard, Albert, *Thomas Hardy: The Novels and Stories*, Cambridge, Mass, Harvard University Press, 1949

Hardy, Barbara, *Thomas Hardy: Imagining Imagination: Hardy's Poetry and Fiction*, London: Athlone Press, 2000

Hirooka, Hideo, *Thomas Hardy's Use of Dialect*, Tokyo: Shinozaki Shorin, 1983

Howe, Irving, *Thomas Hardy,* New York: Macmillan, 1967*

Ingham, Patricia, *Thomas Hardy: A Feminist Reading*, Hemel Hempstead: Harvester, 1989

Jann, Rosemary, "Hardy's Rustics and the Construction of Class", *Victorian Literature and Culture* 28:2 (2000): 411-25

Keith, W.J., *Regions of the Imagination: The Development of British Rural Fiction*, University of Toronto Press, 1988

Kerr, Barbara, *Bound to the Soil: A Social History of Dorset*, Wakefield: EP Publishing, 1975

Radford, Andrew, *Thomas Hardy and the Survivals of Time*, Aldershot: Ashgate, 2003

Wright, Terry, ed, *Thomas Hardy on Screen*, Cambridge University Press, 2005

Zeitler, Michael, *Representations of Culture: Thomas Hardy's Wessex and Victorian Anthropology*, New York: Peter Lang, 2007

# INDEX

First published in 2014 by
Connell Guides
Artist House
35 Little Russell Street
London WC1A 2HH

10 9 8 7 6 5 4 3 2 1

Picture credits:
p.15 © National Portrait Gallery, London
p.29 © Everett Collection/REX
p.51 © Mortimer Rare Book Room, Smith College
p.60 & p.75 © Everett Collection/REX
p.89 © SNAP/REX

A CIP catalogue record for this book is available from the British Library.
ISBN 978-1-907776-15-1

Design © Nathan Burton
Assistant Editors:
Katie Sanderson, Paul Woodward & Pierre Smith Khanna

Printed in Italy by LEGO

www.connellguides.com